DATE DUE

LEARNING
HOW TO MEAN
*Explorations
in the Development of Language*

M.A.K. Halliday

ELSEVIER
NEW YORK OXFORD AMSTERDAM

ELSEVIER NORTH-HOLLAND, INC.
52 Vanderbilt Avenue, New York, NY 10017

First published 1975
by Edward Arnold (Publishers) Ltd.

Elsevier North-Holland edition
published in 1977

Calligraphy in cover design adapted from
Calligraphy by Arthur Baker. © 1973 by Arthur Baker.
Published by Dover Publications, Inc.

Library of Congress Cataloging in Publication Data

Halliday, Michael Alexander Kirkwood.
    Learning how to mean: explorations in the development
    of language

    Bibliography: p.
    1. Children—Language. I. Title
P118.H3   1977   401'.9   76-51756
ISBN 0-444-00200-6

Printed in the United States of America

Contents

Publisher's Introduction

This book, *Learning How to Mean: Explorations in the Development of Language* by M.A.K. Halliday, is part of a series entitled *Explorations in Language Study* published in Great Britain by Edward Arnold Limited under the general editorship of Peter Doughty and Geoffrey Thornton. We are publishing selected books from this series because of the importance and relevance of the material to American educators. Other volumes available for sale from Elsevier include *Explorations in the Functions of Language*, also by M.A.K. Halliday, and *Language Study: The School and the Community*, which comprises three previously published essays in the series by Peter Doughty, Geoffrey Thornton, and Anne Doughty. Additional volumes in *Explorations in Language Study* will be forthcoming.

Foreword

In the course of our efforts to develop a linguistic focus for work in English language, now published as *Language in Use*, we came to realize the extent of the growing interest in what we would call a linguistic approach to language. Lecturers in Colleges and Departments of Education see the relevance of such an approach in the education of teachers. Many teachers in schools and in colleges of Further Education see themselves that 'Educational failure is primarily *linguistic* failure', and have turned to Linguistic Science for some kind of exploration and practical guidance. Many of those now exploring the problems of relationships, community or society, from a sociological or psychological point of view wish to make use of a linguistic approach to the language in so far as it is relevant to these problems.

We were conscious of the wide divergence between the aims of the linguist, primarily interested in language as a system for organizing 'meanings,' and the needs of those who now wanted to gain access to the insights that resulted from that interest. In particular, we were aware of the wide gap that separated the literature of academic Linguistics from the majority of those who wished to find out what Linguistic Science might have to say about language and use of language.

Out of this experience emerged our own view of that much-used term, 'Language Study', developed initially in the chapters of *Exploring Language*, and now given expression in this series. Language Study is not a subject, but a process, which is why the series is to be called *Explorations in Language Study*. Each exploration is focused upon a meeting point between the insights of Linguistic Science, often in conjunction with other social sciences, and the linguistic questions raised by the study of a particular aspect of individual behaviour or human society.

Initially, the volumes in the series have a particular relevance to the role of language in teaching and learning. The editors intend that they should make a basic contribution to the literature of Language Study, doing justice equally to the findings of the academic disciplines involved and the practical needs of those who now want to take a linguistic view of their own particular problems of language and the use of language.

Peter Doughty
Geoffrey Thornton

Acknowledgments

This book incorporates material previously written in the form of articles. Chapter 2 is from "Early language learning: a sociolinguistic approach", a paper presented to the Ninth International Congress of Anthropological & Ethnological Sciences, Chicago, September 1973, and appearing in William C. McCormack & Stephen Wurm (eds.), *Language and Man*, The Hague: Mouton & Co. Chapters 1 and 3 are from "Learning how to mean", prepared as Theoretical Introduction to the section "Studies in productive language", in Part II, Language Development in Healthy Children, of Eric & Elizabeth Lenneberg (eds.), *Foundations of Language Development: a multidisciplinary approach*, UNESCO & International Brain Research Organization. Chapter 4 is "A sociosemiotic perspective on language development," published in *Bulletin of the School of Oriental & African Studies* Vol 37 Pt. 1, 1974 (*In Memory of Wilfred H. Whiteley*). The first part of Chapter 6 is based on sections of "Talking one's way in: a sociolinguistic perspective on language and learning", a paper presented to the "Language & Learning" Seminar of the Scottish Council for Research in Education, January 1973, and appearing in Alan Davie (ed.) *Problems of Language and Learning*, Heinemann Educational Books Ltd, 1975, published in association with Social Science Research Council. Chapter 5, and the latter part of Chapter 6, are entirely new. The author wishes to thank the publishers and editors of the above volumes for their consent to the use of this material in the present context.

Much of the work for this book was done during the author's tenure of a fellowship at the Center for Advanced Study in the Behavioral Sciences, Stanford, California. The author wishes to express his gratitude to the trustees and administrators of the Center for the opportunities which this afforded.

Introduction

Learning How to Mean is the second volume of Michael Halliday's papers to appear in this series. When the first volume appeared, there was some suggestion that work of this kind was inappropriate to the series, because it lay within the territory of 'linguistics'. The publication of the second volume is therefore an opportunity to make more explicit why work of this kind is so essentially a part of the scope of the series.

In the General Introduction to the series, and in my contribution to *Language Study, the Teacher and the Learner*, it is made clear that 'Language Study' is *not* a new 'subject', but a convenient label for a process by which whatever work is relevant can be brought to bear upon particular questions concerned with language in education. 'Language Study' is, therefore, an encouragement to think in terms of questions, and what would be relevant to their being answered, rather than academic boundaries, and how they should be maintained. Consequently, the volumes in the series embrace a wide range of themes, and individual volumes very often do not fit neatly into the pre-existing categories of academic study. Likewise the demands made upon the reader vary from the modest to the very severe, because 'the reader' is no one person, but a very wide range of individuals actively engaged in the exploration of language. Some volumes, like *Language and Community*, or *Language in the Junior School*, meet the reader at the point where he is coming to terms with the fact that he needs to know more about this language business. Others, such as the present volume and its predecessor, say something so important about the nature and function of language that it ought to be made readily available to an audience much, much wider than that of the specialist journal, whatever its intrinsic difficulty.

There is a more important reason, however, for including work at this level in the scope of the series. If the series was not open to original work of this kind, then the concept of 'Language Study' it seeks to exemplify would be deprived of a vital element, an energizing contact with what is new and suggestive. Such work forces us to reconsider the established positions which so often provide the staple content of syllabuses. It encourages us to learn to live dangerously, open to what will alter, perhaps radically alter, what we have previously held to be the case. It reminds us that the questions raised by our study of how human beings use language to live and to learn, and how they learn the language they need, do not fit neatly into our existing gridiron of academic subjects, are not susceptible of tidy answers, and necessarily push us out towards areas where, as yet, our only true knowledge is the extent of our ignorance.

The excitement and the value of this present volume is that it shows how productive it can be to think in terms of questions rather than territories; to think in terms of what kinds of evidence are relevant to the enquiry rather than what kinds of data can best be used as numerical props to the argument; and to think in terms of where the logic of the enquiry must lead rather than what areas are considered safe to enter.

How a child learns his language is the basic question the papers in this volume set out to answer. As Halliday points out, there is more than a simple matter of choice of phrase between 'learning a language' and 'acquiring a language'. To talk of 'language acquisition' is to imply that there is a something 'out there', usually conceived of in terms of the structures of the adult language, which the child must add to its possessions, while remaining itself neutral to the process involved. Alternatively, to talk of *learning* language is to put the emphasis upon the process itself and to see the child as an active participant in the process. As one reads these papers, the implication grows stronger that we would do even better to talk of a child 'making its language', creating out of the total resources its mother tongue has available, semantic, syntactic and phonological, a language system for itself, a system the properties of which it shares with all other speakers of the same language, but yet a system which is unique to its own experience of languaging.

If we adopt this perspective on the child learning its language, however, we are seeing the child as an active agent in creating meaning for itself out of its encounter with the people and events of its experience. Inevitably, it leads us to ask what relationship there might be between the meanings it discovers in the world of its experience and the meanings it makes in the process of learning a language. If we ask how a child *learns* his language, we cannot avoid going on to ask how it is that he learns his culture in the process of learning his language. Perhaps the single most important thing about these papers is that they show how we can begin to answer this question by adopting a functional view of language, a view which relates the 'context of situation', the meanings made manifest in the act of creating text, spoken or written, to the 'context of culture', the meanings manifested in the social system, the environment of 'social man'.

The exploration of these two fundamental questions about "learning how to mean" give rise to many others. Let me note four of these specifically, questions which relate most closely to the problems of those who are concerned with language in its educational context. Firstly, what is it that the child learns as language? What seems most important here is the emphasis upon the functions which a child employs to set up a system for making meanings rather than the structures which a child uses in order to make those meanings manifest in text.

This question will necessarily lead us to ask, what relationship may exist between the child's language and adult language. Should we see it as an imperfect form of the adult language or a system in its own terms, or can we view it in such a way that the limitations of both these perspectives are avoided? "The earliest language" and "Learning how to mean" suggest that we can, in so far as we grasp that "At 10½ months ... (a child has) a language, consisting of a meaning potential in each of the four functions"; that the child's language system ". . . evolves along the familiar lines of generalization followed by abstraction . . ." into the adult language system; and that it is necessary for our account of this process to show how this evaluation comes about.

Given that we are to talk about learning a language as "learning how to mean", we will then be led to ask how a child makes meanings by using language. In order to answer this question adequately Halliday shows that, firstly, we must accept a model of language which contains three levels of organization, sound, form and meaning, not two only, sound and form, with its emphasis upon form as structure, or sound and meaning, with its emphasis upon the relationship between language and thought. Secondly, specifically in "Language development as a semiotic process", he shows why, and in what sense, we must go outside an analysis of the language system itself for an adequate answer to this question, because ". . . a child, in the act of learning language is also learning the culture through language. The semantic system which he is constructing becomes the primary mode of transmission of the culture". In order to make sense of this process we must seek something 'outside language' parallel to, and in close interaction with, this semantic system. Michael Halliday suggests we use ". . . the social system considered as a system of meanings", in other words, the concept of a *social semiotic*, a concept which systematizes our own intuition that each man's relationship to his human environment is not empty, but full of meaning for him, and that this meaning has been learnt through his interaction with others in that environment.

And this brings me to my fourth and final question. If the source of the 'meaning potential' the child builds up in the process of creating a language system for himself is the social system in which he participates, what are these 'meanings' that the social system makes available to him, and how do they manifest themselves in actual text, his local and particular *use* of his language system? What Michael Halliday demonstrates is that the answer to this most taxing of questions is to be found in the way in which a language system is organized *as a system for making meanings* rather than a device for generating structures. In "Language development as a semiotic process", he says that:

Because all our linguistic acts, as adults, are mediated by the ideational and interpersonal systems, *which are at the centre of the language system we create for ourselves* (my italics) every act is not only linguistic, a use of the potential of the language system, but social and cultural, an expression of who we are and what we gave value to.

In "Into adult language", he shows how the child pursues his process of ". . . generalization followed by abstraction", to the point where he can organize his 'meaning potential' in terms of two very broad functions:

. . . the mathetic function, that of language as learning, that creates the conditions for the development of ideational meanings, those expressing the speaker's experience of the phenomena around and inside him. . . and the pragmatic function, that of language as doing, that creates the conditions for the development of interpersonal meanings, those expressing the speaker's role in and angle on the communication process.

In "The social context of language development", he considers how the child uses his language to construct for himself "an interpretative model of the environment in which he finds himself", that is, how the child constructs for himself a perspective on reality through the very process of constructing a language for himself. I think I can sum up the central importance of this volume for the series, and for 'Language Study', and for the whole question of language in the educational context by one last quotation:

"... language is both a product of, and the means by which we have access to, the systems of meaning relationship that constitute culture, the specifically human environment".

That the child makes a language system for himself out of his cumulative experience of "the specifically human environment" to which he has access is a fact that no one working in education can now afford to ignore or evade.

Peter Doughty

Note on the transcriptions

Nigel's expressions in Phase I, and also early Phase II, are written in the International Phonetic Alphabet. The form is given as it appears in my notes, sometimes slightly regularized but not so much as to obscure the variation that typically occurs.

Intonation, since it is such a fundamental aspect of the young child's linguistic system, is marked throughout; the symbols used are:

   \ falling tone   (approximates to adult tone 1)
   / rising tone   (,,   ,,   tones 2 and 3)
  ∨ falling-rising tone (,,   ,,   tone 4)
  ∧ rising-falling tone (,,   ,,   tone 5)
   – (close to letter symbol, thus: ā) level tone, mid or low
   – (raised above letter symbol, thus: ā) level tone, high

In continuous passages, a figure in parenthesis following a sentence refers to the number of repetitions of that sentence on that occasion. When the sentence was repeated a large number of times, the form (repet.) is used.

1 Language development studies

1. Learning the mother tongue: knowledge or interaction?

Considered in the perspective of language development as a whole, the latest period of intensive study in this field—the last decade or more—has been characterized by what may, in time, come to seem a rather one-sided concentration on grammatical structure. The question that has most frequently been asked is, 'How does the child acquire structure?' Martin Braine, for example, writing in 1971, introduces his comprehensive survey of work on 'the acquisition of language' with the words '. . . this review is concerned only with the acquisition of linguistic structure. Thus, work on child language where the concern is with social or intellectual development will not be reviewed. Even within the area defined, the subject of lexical development will be reviewed only very sketchily'. No mention is made of the development of the semantic system.

The implication has been that the learning of structure is really the heart of the language learning process. And it is perhaps not too far-fetched to recognize in the use of the term *acquisition*, a further implication that structure, and therefore language itself, is a commodity of some kind that the child has to gain possession of in the course of maturation.

The dominant standpoint has been a psycholinguistic one; and the dominant issue, at least in the United States where much of the most important work has been carried out, has been that between 'nativist' and 'environmentalist' interpretations, although there seems to be no necessary connection between these as general philosophical positions on the one hand and the particular models of the processes involved in the learning of linguistic structure that have been most typically associated with them on the other. The nativist view makes the assumption that human beings possess an innate capacity that is specific to language learning. It does not follow from this assumption that the child necessarily learns language by setting up hypothetical rules of grammar and matching them against what he hears; but there has been a widely-held interpretation along these lines. Environmentalist views, by contrast, emphasize the aspect of language learning which relates it to other learning tasks, and assume its dependence on environmental conditions. This, again, is often taken to imply an associationist, stimulus-response model of the learning process, although there is no essential connection between the two.

In the investigation of how the child learns grammatical structure, attention has naturally been focussed on the nature of the earliest structural combinations which the child produces for himself, where he puts together two or more elements—typically but not necessarily words—which on other occasions he uses in isolation, or in other combinations. There are in principle two ways of looking at these combinations, the one adult-oriented and the other child-oriented. The child's structures may be represented either as approximations to the forms of adult language, or as independent structures sui generis. The first approach, which is in a sense presupposed if one adopts a nativist view, involves treating many of the child's utterances, perhaps all of them at a certain stage, as ill-formed; they are interpreted as deviations from an eventual norm, resulting from distortions of various kinds, particularly the deletion of elements. This brings out their relationship to the adult forms; but it blocks the way to the recognition and interpretation of the child's own system. In the second approach, the child's earliest structures are analyzed as combinations of elements forming a system in their own right, typically a system that is based on the contrast between closed and open-ended classes; the best-known example of this is Braine's 'pivotal' model, with its categories of 'pivot' and 'open'. Such an analysis has been criticized on the grounds that it fails to account for ambiguous forms. There is a well-known example cited by Lois Bloom, of the child who uses the combination mummy sock in two quite different meanings, (i) 'mummy's sock', (ii) 'mummy is putting my socks on'; the analysis would fail to show any difference between the two. But this is an aspect of a more general limitation, namely that the interpretation of structure in these child-oriented terms does not account for the meaning of what the

2

child says. Nor does it easily suggest how, or why, the child moves from his own system into the adult system: if language development is primarily the acquisition of structure, why does the child learn one set of structures in order to discard them in favour of another? There is an excellent discussion of these and related issues in a new book by Roger Brown, entitled *A First Language*.

None of the above objections is very serious provided it is recognized, first, that structural analysis is a highly abstract exercise, in which both types of representation are valid and each affords its own insight; and secondly—a related point—that language development is much more than the acquisition of structure. But, by the same token, the form in which the grammatical structures of the child's language are represented is then no longer the central issue. The fundamental question is, 'How does the child learn language?'. In other words, how does he master the adult linguistic system—in which grammar is just one part, and structure is just one part of grammar? How does he build up a multiple coding system consisting of content, form, and expression: a system of meaning relations, together with their realization as configurations of words and structures and the realization of these in turn as phonological patterns?

These questions are brought up in what Roger Brown calls a 'rich interpretation' of children's language: an approach to language development through the investigation of meaning. The interpretation of first language learning in semantic terms is not, of course, a new idea; there is a long history of such work. But when the psychologists' traditional two-level model of language (as consisting of sound and meaning) came to be overtaken by the model provided by structuralist linguistics—which was still in terms of two levels, but this time of sound and form—it rather receded into the background. Just how far the latter view came to prevail can be seen in the following quotation from Ervin and Miller: 'The most important contribution that modern linguistics has brought to child language studies is the conception of what a language is. A language is a system that can be described internally in terms of two primary parts or levels—the phonological (sound system) and the grammatical. A complete description of a language would include an account of all possible phonological sequences and also a set of rules by which we can predict all the possible sentences in that language'.

It is now generally recognized that the adult language system is basically tri-stratal in nature—that it consists of sound, form and

3

meaning. Prague School theory, glossematics, system-structure theory, tagmemics, stratification theory and the later versions of transformation theory are all variants on this theme. As a result, the semantic perspective has been restored. The 'rich interpretation' may still rest on a structural analysis of the utterances of children's speech; but if so, this is an analysis at the semological level in which the elements of structure are functional in character and therefore clearly related to the meaning. Most typical of this approach would be a structural analysis in terms of the transitivity functions of the clause, functions such as Agent and Process. But it is worth commenting here that all functional categories in grammar, whether those of transitivity, like Fillmore's 'cases', or those of thematic structure, like topic and comment, and including traditional 'purely grammatical' ones like subject and modifier, are semantic in origin. All of them could figure appropriately in a semantic interpretation of linguistic structure.

The approach to structure through meaning may also be either child-oriented or adult-oriented. For example, the utterance <u>now room</u> (see p. 103), which could be glossed as 'now let's go to (play in) (daddy's) room', could be analyzed on the adult model as something like Imperative + Process + Agent + Locative + Temporal, with Imperative, Process and Agent deleted; or else, in its own terms, as something like Request for joint action + Arena, with nothing omitted or 'understood'.

Once again, these are abstract representations and neither can be said to be wrong. But a child-oriented semantic analysis of the latter kind, which is very suggestive, carries certain further implications. Since the elements of the structure are not being explained as (approximations to) those of the adult language, there is presumably some other source from which they are derived and in terms of which they have any meaning. Why, for example, would we postulate an element such as 'Request for joint action'? This is explicable only if one of the functions of language is to call for action on the part of others, to regulate their behaviour in some way. No doubt this is true; but to make it explicit implies some specification of the total set of functions of language, some kind of a functional hypothesis which is not just a list of uses of language but a system of developmental functions from each of which a range of meanings, or 'meaning potential', is derived.

4

2. A functional—interactional approach

At this point the attempt to understand the structure of the child's utterances leads us directly into questions about the linguistic system as a whole, and specifically questions about the functions for which that system first develops. There is an important link between the two senses of 'function', the first as in 'functions in structure' and the second as in 'functions of language': the former, when interpreted semantically, imply the latter. The functional roles that combine to make up a linguistic structure, such as Agent + Process + Goal + Location, reflect the particular function of language that that structure has evolved to serve—in this case the interpretation of experience of the external world.

But whether or not the line of approach is through considerations of structure, once the interest is focussed on how the child learns a system of meanings this points to some kind of investigation in functional terms. It becomes necessary to look beyond the language itself, but at the same time to do so without presupposing a particular conceptual framework, because this is precisely what the child is using language to construct; and herein lies the value of a functional approach. Early language development may be interpreted as the child's progressive mastery of a functional potential.

There is yet a further implication here, one which takes us into the social foundations of language. If, for example, language is used, from an early stage, to regulate the behaviour of others, and it is suggested that the mastery of this function is one of the essential steps in the developmental process, this assumes some general framework of social structure and social processes in terms of which a function such as 'regulatory' would make sense. More particularly—since we are concerned with the language of the child—it presupposes a concept of cultural transmission within which the role of language in the transmission process may be highlighted and defined. Here the concept of meaning, and of learning to mean, is in the last analysis interpreted in sociological terms, in the context of some chain of dependence such as: social order—transmission of the social order to the child—role of language in the transmission process—functions of language in relation to this role—meanings derived from these functions.

In this way the functional interpretation of the child's meanings implies a sociolinguistic approach, in which the learning of the mother tongue is interpreted as a process of interaction between the child and other human beings. From this perspective, which is complementary to the psycholinguistic one, not in any sense contradictory, the focus of attention is on the linguistic system as a whole, considered as having a (functionally organized) meaning potential, or a semantic system, at one end, and a vocal potential, or phonological system, at the other. In this context, structure no longer occupies the centre of the stage; it enters in because it is one form of the realization of meanings.

This has certain important consequences for the investigation of language development. The analysis does not depend on utterances of more than one element, that is, on combinations of words as structural units. This is particularly significant because, although the word in the sense of a lexical item or lexeme (i.e. vocabulary) soon comes to play an essential part in the development of the child's linguistic system, the word as a structural unit, which is a different concept, does not, or does so much less prominently. A word in this latter sense is merely one type of constituent among others; and the young child has no special awareness of words as constituents, any more than he has of groups or clauses. From the functional point of view, as soon as there are meaningful expressions there is language, and the investigation can begin at a time before words and structures have evolved to take over the burden of realization.

It then emerges that the child already has a linguistic system before he has any words or structures at all. He is capable of expressing a considerable range of meanings, meanings which at first seem difficult to pin down, because they do not translate easily into adult language, but which become quite transparent when interpreted functionally, in the light of the question "What has the child learnt to do by means of language?' The transition from this phase into the adult system can also be explained in functional terms, although it becomes necessary to modify the concept of function very considerably in passing from the developmental origins of the system, where 'function' equals 'use', to the highly abstract sense in which we can talk of the functional organization of the adult language. However, this modification in the concept 'function of language' is itself one of the major sources of insight into the process whereby the adult system evolves from that of the child.

In what follows we shall suggest a tentative framework for a functional, or sociolinguistic, account of the early development of the mother tongue. We shall postulate three phases in this

6

development: Phase I, the child's initial functional-linguistic system; Phase II, the transition from this system to that of the adult language; Phase III, the learning of the adult language.

The account we are offering does not presuppose any one particular psychological model of language acquisition or theory of learning. Linguistically, it assumes some form of a realizational model of language; the descriptive techniques are those of system-structure theory, derived from Firth, with the 'system' as the basic concept. (A system is defined as a set of options with a condition of entry: that is, it is a range of alternatives which may be behavioural, semantic, grammatical etc., together with a specification of the environment in which selection must be made among these alternatives. It has the form 'If x, then either a or b or . . . '.) This form of representation can be readily interpreted in other terms, especially in terms of stratification theory as developed by Lamb and Reich. The sociological standpoint is derived from the findings and the theoretical work of Bernstein. The particular impetus for the detailed study of a developing language system, which provides the observational basis for this sketch, came from working over a number of years with teachers of English as a mother tongue, who were attempting to grapple with the fundamental problem of language in education. Their experience showed me that we are still far from understanding the essential patterns of language development in the pre-school child, in the deeper sense of being able to answer the question, "How does a child learn to mean?"

2 The earliest language

1. Language as meaning potential

We shall begin by considering the child's learning of his first language in the period extending roughly from six to eighteen months of age. Our approach to this will be through semantics; the learning of language will be interpreted as the learning of a system of meanings. A child who is learning his first language is learning how to mean; in this perspective, the linguistic system is to be seen as a semantic potential. It is a range of possible meanings; together with the means whereby these meanings are realized, or expressed.

The viewpoint that we are taking is a functional one. We shall relate the meaning, in turn, to linguistic function, to the functions that language is made to serve in the life of the growing child. There are two reasons for looking at it in this way. The first is that the functional approach is of value in its own right, in that it gives us insight into the reasons why the child takes the steps he does. If we have a functional viewpoint, we may be able to suggest why it is that the child builds up the system in the particular way he does: why, for example, there comes a point where he has to take over the adult language, and to build certain of its features, such as structure and vocabulary, into his total potential. The second reason for looking at the process from a functional point of view is that it also gives us some insight into why the adult language has evolved in the way it has. The human brain would have been capable of constructing a hundred and one different types of semiotic system; why is it that language evolved in this particular way as a semiotic system with the particular properties that it has? If we examine this question developmentally, we can see that the adult linguistic system is structured in a way which reflects very closely its functional origins.

The term semantic is not to be understood in the restricted

sense of 'lexicosemantic', i.e. concerned with the meanings of words. It refers to the totality of meaning in language, whether such meaning is encoded in the form of vocabulary or not. A child cannot learn word meanings unless he also has words— that is, an organized vocabulary, not necessarily in the phonological shapes of the adult lexicon. But it is our contention that the learning of language is essentially the learning of a semantic system, and that this process is already well under weigh before the child has any words at all. He learns to mean long before he adopts the lexical mode for the realization of meanings.

Similarly the term functional is not to be understood in the sense of the specific hypothesis that the child interprets the names of objects by reference to the functions of these objects, or that he learns word classes by reference to the structural functions (for example, agent of a transitive verb) which reflect the potentialities of objects in the real world. It refers to the general notion that the child learns language as a system of meanings in functional contexts, these contexts becoming, in turn, the principle of organization of the adult semantic system (as this is recognized in 'functional' theories of language).

There is still relatively little literature on the early period, before eighteen months or so; probably because it is quite difficult during this period to recognize that the process of language learning is taking place at all. This is the period before the child has really started to use the adult language as his model. It might be said, in fact, that the language that is learnt at this stage owes nothing at all to the adult language that the child hears around him. This would be an oversimplification, since in fact the child *may* use imitations of the adult phonology as part of the resources for expressing his meaning. But equally he may not; and the point is that it does not matter at this stage whether he does or not.

Children vary enormously at this age in the extent to which they attempt to construct some kind of imitative phonological system. It is not entirely clear why they vary in this way; presumably, partly because of differences in their innate ability to imitate adult speech sounds and partly because of differences in the environment—not only how much speech they hear, but also, and perhaps more important, from how many different people, how much from adults and how much from other children, how much is addressed to them, how much their own efforts are reinforced, and so on. And also, no doubt, because of differences in personality; children differ very much as regards how they respond to

other people's reaction to their own efforts, how far they are per-
fectionists—there are some children who appear simply not to
attempt things, at least in public, until they are satisfied with
their own performance. So there may be all sorts of factors con-
tributing to the very noticeable difference among children at this
age, when some of them attempt a great deal of phonetic imitation,
and others practically none.

In both these cases there is a source of difficulty for the investigator. If the child does imitate the phonology of the adult language,
then one is inclined to use this as the criterion for deciding whether
his sounds are linguistic or not, whereas it is really not the relevant
point. His own system is a system of meanings, and some or all of
these meanings may be expressed through sounds borrowed from
the adult language. On the other hand, it may be that none of
them are, and in that case the investigator tends not to recognize
that there is any language learning taking place at all. In fact
there is; there is a great deal of language learning at this stage.
The child is already both responding to and producing signals of a
linguistic kind.

In the very first instance, he is learning that there is such a thing
as language at all, that vocal sounds are functional in character.
He is learning that the articulatory resources with which he is
endowed can be put to the service of certain functions in his own
life. For a child, using his voice is doing something; it is a form
of action, and one which soon develops its own patterns and its
own significant contexts. On what criteria then do we decide
that the sounds which the child is making do in some sense constitute a linguistic system, if they are not themselves identifiable
as sounds drawn from the adult language—or if they *may* not
be, since as we have said it does not matter at this stage whether
they are or not? Here we have a further reason for adopting a
functional standpoint. As any parent knows, we can observe at
a very early stage, typically perhaps beginning in the period from
six to nine months, that a child begins using vocal sounds con-
sistently and systematically, developing some kind of constant
relation between sounds and meanings. But these meanings are
not something which can be glossed in terms of the adult language,
something which we can enter into a dictionary and which correspond to the meanings of words and phrases and structures in
the adult language. They are meanings which we can best interpret if we begin with some kind of functional hypothesis, a hypothesis about what it is that the child is doing with his voice, what

it is that he is making the speech sounds do for him; in other words, if we recognize that there are certain fundamental goals or purposes that the child achieves through the use of vocal sound. He uses his voice to order people about, to get them to do things for him; he uses it to demand certain objects or services; he uses it to make contact with people, to feel close to them; and so on. All these things are meaningful actions.

2. Data for the present study

I have attempted a fairly intensive study of the language of one particular child beginning at this early stage; and I have compiled a number of descriptions of his language covering the period from nine to eighteen months. It seems odd to refer to these as 'grammars', when the one level that is totally absent from the child's linguistic system at this period is that that we know as grammar: it has neither structure nor vocabulary in it; so let me revert to an earlier terminological practice and call them descriptions. I have written a number of descriptions of this child's language which I think are complete. (If they are, then they are the only complete descriptions of any language that I have ever written or am ever likely to write.) It will be helpful here to say briefly what form these descriptions take and how they were arrived at.

I made notes of the child's utterances, using only the traditional equipment of the field worker, well suited to this stage, a notebook and pencil. I listened in, sometimes taking part in the situation and sometimes staying outside it, hiding behind doors and furniture; and I noted down any meaningful expression that I thought I was observing for the first time. Then I also noted down expressions which I considered to be the same as those I had observed before; not every time I heard them, of course, which would be impossible, but at fairly frequent intervals, the point being that at this stage it is not enough to assume that because some item has been observed to occur it is now part of the child's linguistic system. Language learning at this stage is not a steady advance; like other forms of learning, it has its ups and downs. Elements of the system come and go; they get learnt and they get forgotten, or else modified or altered. For example, for a period of something around four months, the child I was working with, Nigel, had a particular sound which he used for commenting on the presence of an aeroplane flying overhead; and it was a sound which, it is fair to guess, was his imitation of the noise of the aeroplane. After a while, it simply dropped out of the system; and then later on after an interval, a gap of about three months, came another word for an aeroplane which was an imitation of the adult word. I would not, incidentally, regard these two terms as synonymous. The functional meaning of the item which we interpret as 'aeroplane' in the first instance was rather different from the functional meaning of the second one; the semantic system had changed in the interval. Other elements which entered into the system and subsequently disappeared included a number of forms of demand and of response to offers; all these are shown in the accompanying figures (Figures 1–6, pp. 148–157).

Then, at intervals of six weeks, I interpreted these notes into a description of the system, so that the system was reinterpreted and described afresh each six weeks. This seemed to be the optimum interval. If I had chosen a longer period, then certain significant steps in the development would have been left out; whereas if I had chosen a shorter period I would have been at the mercy of random non-occurrences, items which simply had not been observed over the period but which should have been recognized as present in the system. So a month and a half seemed to work out the best for the purpose. This practice I began at nine months, because before the age of nine months Nigel had no system at all; and indeed the very first description represents a stage that I would also regard as prelinguistic, since it does not meet the criteria which I set up for recognizing the presence of a linguistic system. That one I have coded as NL 0, NL standing for 'Nigel's language'; so we have NL 0 at nine months, NL 1 at $10\frac{1}{2}$ months, NL 2 at 12 months, NL 3 at $13\frac{1}{2}$ months, NL 4 at 15 months, NL 5 at $16\frac{1}{2}$ months, and NL 6 at 18 months.

3. The child's first language: content and expression

Now there are certain theoretical considerations which it seems have to be built in to any study of language development at this early stage. These centre around the concepts of what we may call the *content* and the *expression*, or the meaning and the sound. The first point is that these are all there is. That is to say, the child's language system at this stage is a two-level system. It consists of a content and an expression, and each element in the system is a simple sign having just these two aspects: it is a 'content-expression pair'. In other words, the system differs from the adult language system in that it has no intermediate level; it has no stratum of grammar (we should say *lexicogrammar*, since this stratum includes vocabulary) intermediate between the meanings and the sounds. So we shall consider the system as being made up of a content and an expression, and each element in the system as being itself made up of a meaning and a sound.

Secondly, there are certain features that we need to specify about the content and the expression. As far as the expression is concerned, one point has already been made: the particular expressions are not, or at least may not be, imitations of the adult language. In principle, at this stage the expression owes nothing to the adult language at all. It is a system of vocal postures, including the two components of articulation and intonation. If we refer to them as *postures*, this is in order to stress the fact that, for the notation of the expression system, the International Phonetic Alphabet is not really appropriate; as others have pointed out, it is too specific. What one requires is something more in the nature of a prosodic notation, which is postural in exactly this sense; it represents postures which are taken up by the articulatory organs, general configurations rather than the specific bundles of contrastive phonetic features which make up the elements of the adult sound system.

By analogy, we can make the same point about the content. In general, we cannot represent the content of the child's system at this stage in terms of the words and structures of the adult language. We cannot match the child's meanings with the elements of the adult semantic system, which are again too specific. What is needed, in similar fashion, is a kind of postural notation for the content. What does this mean in fact? It means some form of a functional representation of meaning. The content, in other words, has to be specified in relation to the functions of language.

This point needs to be elaborated, in order to explain why we consider that these early vocalizations constitute language. Let us return, first, to the nature of the system itself. It is very clear that we cannot define language at this early stage in terms of either structures or of words. In the first place, there are no structures; each utterance consists of one element only. This is not to imply that an utterance which consists of one element only can never have a structure; there are many items (clause types, phrase types &c.) of the adult language which do consist of one element, and these are undoubtedly structures, so that the utterances which stand as tokens of these types are themselves structured. But one cannot recognize a one-element structure except by reference to the existence of at least some structures of two or more elements, and these are not present in the child's system. There are no two-element utterances; hence there is no structure, and hence we cannot describe language acquisition at this stage in terms of structure, or in terms of any measure, mean length of utterance for example, which implies the presence of structure. In the second place, there are no words. The point has already been made that the child's utterances are not imitations of adult words—they are not words in the sense of items deriving their phonological shape from the English lexicon. Nor, however, are they words in the more important sense of the term, vocabulary items with matching definitions. Putting these two facts together, that there are no structures and that there are no words, we can summarize by saying that the language we are describing has no level of *form*; or, as we expressed it earlier, it does not possess a lexicogrammar, a level of organization consisting of a grammar and a vocabulary.

This would suffice to exclude what a young child constructs from the domain of language, since language is normally defined as a tristratal system, having a semantics, a grammar and a phonology. In the last resort, of course, it does not matter whether we call the system the child develops at this stage language or not, provided we relate it to the total picture of language development. But in order to bring out the underlying continuity between the child's system and that of the adult we can identify those features of the former which show it to be language in the making. What it consists of is a set of content-expression pairs; and this enables us to define one criterion for characterizing and for accepting anything as an element in that system, namely that there should be a constant relation between the content and the expression. Let us give an illustration of this. Whenever, for example, Nigel says nananana it always means something like 'I want that thing now'; and when he expresses the meaning 'I want that thing now' by means of a vocal symbol, he always does so by saying nananana. This meaning-sound relation qualifies, so to speak, as part of a language. Let us refer to this requirement of a constant relation between content and expression as the requirement of *systematicity*.

The other requirement that we can set up on the basis of the child's system is that of *functionality*. In order to qualify as part of a language, the child's vocalizations must be not only systematic but also functional. This means that the content should be such that it can be interpreted by reference to a prior established set of functions. To continue with the same example, the meaning 'I want that thing now' is derivable from one of the functions that we are postulating as the set of original developmental functions from which the child starts, namely the instrumental function, the use of language to satisfy the child's material needs. In other words, there is no system of content as such, in abstraction from the context of situation. There is only content *with respect*; that is, with respect to the functions that language serves in the life of the developing child.

We are not here setting up some arbitrary meanings that are, as it were, floating in the air. We are setting up meanings in terms of certain generalized contexts of language use. The child is learning to be and to do, to act and interact in meaningful ways. He is learning a system of meaningful behaviour; in other words, he is learning a semiotic system. Part of his meaningful action is linguistic. But none of it takes place in isolation; it is always within some social context. So the content of an utterance is the meaning that it has with respect to a given function, to one or other of the things that the child is making language do for him. It is a semiotic act which is interpretable by reference to the total range of semiotic options, the total meaning potential that the child has accessible to him at that moment.

The question then is: what are the functions that we can recognize as determining a child's semiotic system at this stage, and how do we arrive at them? Here we must try to keep things in proportion, shunting between sensible observation on the one hand and imaginative but at the same time goal-directed theory on the other.

On the one hand we can see, ourselves, as any parent can see, what a child is doing when he is uttering speech sounds, and what contributions these speech sounds are making to the total activity in which he is engaged. We have some reasonably clear impression of the function of speech in a context; and we can characterize this very adequately in quite general terms in relation to the child's contexts of situation. In other words, proceeding solely from observation, and using just the amount of commonsense the researcher ought to possess if he did not suspend it while on duty, we could reach generalizations such as 'this child says <u>nananana</u> when he wants to get something handed to him'. And we could arrive at this on a purely inductive basis—or as nearly inductive as one ever gets: the educated adult cannot proceed very far without imposing some kind of theory as he goes along.

On the other hand, while we could draw some interesting conclusions in this way, there would be a very severe limitation on how far we could go. If we want to understand the nature of the developmental process, and in particular to make the bridge between the language that the child creates for himself at the very first stage and the adult language that he comes out with at the end, then we must relate the generalizations that we make about the child's uses of language to some hypothesis about the overall functions of language in the life of social man. It is clear that we will not be able to do this from a purely empirical standpoint, because by the time the child is, say, 2½, we will no longer be able to give any kind of significant general account of his uses of language. By this time, like the adult, he already uses language for so many different purposes that if we try to list them we shall simply get an endless catalogue; or rather, we shall get a whole series of catalogues with no reason for preferring one over another. We have to find some other more theoretical basis for matching the observations about language use with some theoretical construct of a functional nature. And there are two possible sources for this type of a theory of language functions, one from within language itself and one from outside it.

4. Sources of functional concepts

Let us look at each of these briefly in turn. If we consider first the linguistic system itself, we find that the adult language displays certain features which can only be interpreted in functional terms. These are found, naturally, in the area of meaning: the semantic system of the adult language is very clearly functional in its composition. It reflects the fact that language has evolved in the service of certain particular human needs. But what is really significant is that this functional principle is carried over and built in to the grammar, so that the internal organization of the grammatical system is also functional in character.

If we consider language as a meaning potential, an open-ended and theoretically infinite range of options in meaning, then we find that these options are grouped into a very small number of sets such that each set of options is subject to strong internal constraints but weak external constraints. In other words, when the speaker makes selections in the system (which are essentially selections in meaning), a choice that he makes in one set of options has a great deal of effect on the other choices that he makes within the same set, but practically no effect on the choices he makes among the options in the other sets. These sets of options constitute the functional components of the semantic system.

Broadly speaking we can characterize these functional components as follows. First, there are the *ideational* options, those relating to the content of what is said. With this component, the speaker expresses his experience of the phenomena of the external world, and of the internal world of his own consciousness. This is what we might call the *observer* function of language, language as a means of talking about the real world. It also includes a subcomponent concerned with the expression of logical relations which are first perceived and interpreted by the child as relations between things.

Secondly, there is the *interpersonal* component of the semantic system, reflecting the function of language as a means whereby the speaker participates in the speech situation. This we may call the *intruder* function of language. Through the options in this component, the speaker adopts a role, or a set of roles, vis-à-vis the participants in the speech situation, and also assigns roles to the other participants, while accepting (or rejecting) those that are assigned to him; he expresses his own judgments, his own attitudes, his own personality, and in so doing exerts certain effects on the hearers. These have been known as the 'expressive-conative' functions of language. The options that the speaker takes up in this area of meaning, while they are strongly interrelated among one another, are in large measure independent of the options which he takes up of an ideational kind, those under the first heading.

And then, finally, there is a third semantic function which is in a sense an enabling function, one without which the other two could not be put into effect; this we shall refer to as the *textual* function, the function that language has of creating text. It is through the options in this component that the speaker is enabled to make what he says operational in the context, as distinct from being merely citational, like lists of words in a dictionary, or sentences in a grammar book. The textual function we can regard as being that which breathes life into language; in another metaphor, it provides texture, and without texture there is no text.

We can take account of this functional organization of the semantic system of the adult language in helping us to determine what are likely to be the developmental functions from which the child starts. Somehow the child moves from the one to the other, from his own system to that of the adult; and our hypothesis must be such as at least to show that it would have been possible for him to make the transition. Ideally, of course, we would like it to be rather stronger, in the sense that it should show some clear motivation why the child should move into the adult language as the means of extending the functional potential that he already has. All this is looking at the question from inside language.

Outside language, we turn to some kind of social theory that accommodates language as an essential element, and in particular one that embodies some notion of what are the functional contexts of language use that are likely to be critical for the child. Here the most obviously relevant work is that of Basil Bernstein, whose theory of social structure and social change embodies a concept of cultural transmission within which he has been able to identify a number of what he calls 'critical socializing contexts', types of situation involving the use of language which play a key part in the transmission of culture to the child. Bernstein has identified a certain number of such contexts in what amounts to a sociological theory of linguistic functions. At one point he enumerates four such contexts, which he refers to as the regulative, the instructional, the imaginative or innovative, and the interpersonal. The fact that in Bernstein's work language is the central factor in cultural transmission makes it likely that contexts which Bernstein recognizes as critical for cultural transmission will also be critical in the language learning process.

5. Phase I functions

We can now put together the various strands that make up a pattern of thinking about language in functional terms. In the first place, there are the observations relating to the use of language by a very small child. In the second place, there are the theoretical considerations about linguistic function; and these theories include, in turn, first those which are essentially linguistic in nature, functional theories of language and of the semantic system, and secondly those which are essentially extra-linguistic in nature, sociological theories embodying some concept of cultural transmission and processes of socialization. Taking these factors into account I had suggested a set of functions which would serve for the interpretation of the language of a very young child; that is, as an initial hypothesis for some kind of functional or sociolinguistic approach to early language development. The postulated set of functions was as follows:

18

(1) Instrumental
(2) Regulatory
(3) Interactional
(4) Personal
(5) Heuristic
(6) Imaginative

Let me comment briefly on each of these.

(1) The *instrumental* function is the function that language serves of satisfying the child's material needs, of enabling him to obtain the goods and services that he wants. This is the 'I want' function of language; and it is likely to include a general expression of desire, some element meaning simply "I want that object there (present in the context)," as well as perhaps other expressions relating to specific desires, responses to questions "Do you want . . .?" and so on.

(2) The *regulatory* function is related to this, but it is also distinct. It is the function of language as controlling the behaviour of others, something which the child recognizes very easily because language is used on him in this way: language is used to control his own behaviour and he soon learns that he can turn the tables and use it to control others. The regulatory is the 'do as I tell you' function of language. The difference between this and the instrumental is that in the instrumental the focus is on the goods or services required and it does not matter who provides them, whereas regulatory utterances are directed towards a particular individual, and it is the behaviour of that individual that is to be influenced. Typically therefore this function includes meanings such as, again, a generalized request "Do that," meaning "Do what you have just been doing (in the context)", "Do that again"; as well as various specific demands, particularly in the form of suggestions "Let's do . . .," such as "Let's go for a walk," "Let's play this game," "Let's sing a song" and so forth.

(3) The *interactional* function is what we might gloss as the 'me and you' function of language. This is language used by the child to interact with those around him, particularly his mother and others that are important to him, and it includes meanings such as generalized greetings "Hello," "Pleased to see you," and also responses to calls "Yes?", as well as more specific forms. For example, the first names of particular individuals that the child learns are typically used with a purely interactional function; and there may be other specific meanings of an interactional kind

involving the focussing of attention on particular objects in the environment, some favourite objects of the child which are used as channels for interacting with those around him.

(In view of the great variety in young children's use of the mummy and daddy forms, and the continuing discussion around the question whether they are or are not proper names, it should be made clear that in Nigel's system these items functioned unequivocally as proper names: they were used only interactionally (and never, for example, as expression of a demand), and were attached from the start uniquely to specific individuals. The forms themselves had the distinctive phonological shape that Nigel reserved for proper names, and no instance was noted of their use in any other context. See Figures 2–5, pp. 149–155.)

(4) Fourthly there is the *personal* function. This is language used to express the child's own uniqueness; to express his awareness of himself, in contradistinction to his environment, and then to mould that self—ultimately, language in the development of the personality. This includes, therefore, expressions of personal feelings, of participation and withdrawal, of interest, pleasure, disgust and so forth, and extends later on to more specific intrusion of the child as a personality into the speech situation. We might call this the 'here I come' function of language.

(5) Fifthly, once the boundary between the child himself and his environment is beginning to be recognized, then the child can turn towards the exploration of the environment; this is the *heuristic* function of language, the 'tell me why' function, that which later on develops into the whole range of questioning forms that the young child uses. At this very early stage, in its most elementary form the heuristic use of language is the demand for a name, which is the child's way of categorizing the objects of the physical world; but it soon expands into a variety of more specific meanings.

(6) Finally we have the *imaginative* function, which is the function of language whereby the child creates an environment of his own. As well as moving into, taking over and exploring the universe which he finds around him, the child also uses language for creating a universe of his own, a world initially of pure sound, but which gradually turns into one of story and make-believe and let's-pretend, and ultimately into the realm of poetry and imaginative writing. This we may call the 'let's pretend' function of language.

Later on there is in fact a seventh to be added to the list; but the initial hypothesis was that this seventh function, although it is the one which is undoubtedly dominant in the adult's use of language, and even more so in the adult's image of what language is, is one which does not emerge in the life of a child until considerably after the others. This is the one that we can call the *informative* function of language, the 'I've got something to tell you' function. The idea that language can be used as a means of communicating information to someone who does not already possess that information is a very sophisticated one which depends on the internalization of a whole complex set of linguistic concepts that the young child does not possess. It is the only purely intrinsic function of language, the only use of language in a function that is definable solely by reference to language. And it is one which is not present at all in the phase of language development which we are considering here. In Nigel's case, for example, it did not begin to appear until a much later stage, round about 22 months. It is useful, however, to refer to it at this point, particularly because it tends to predominate in adult thinking about language. This, in fact, is one of the reasons why the adult finds it so difficult to interpret the image of language that a very young child has internalized. The young child has a very clear notion of the functions of his own linguistic system. He knows very well what he can do with it. But what he can do with it is not at all the same thing as what the adult does, still less as what he thinks he does, with his linguistic system.

These, then, are the initial functions with respect to which we identify the content of what the child is learning to say, the meanings that are present in this very early linguistic system. All those utterances which we identify as language can be interpreted in the light of some such set of functions as these. Within each one of these functions, we shall recognise a range of alternatives, of options in meaning, that the child has mastered at this particular stage; this is the set of possibilities that is open and accessible to him in this particular function of language.

It is this notion of a range of alternatives, a set of options, that provides the foundation of a functional approach to early language development. Somewhat surprisingly, perhaps, the distinction between what is and what is not part of the child's linguistic system proves to be quite easy to draw at this stage; at least, I found it so. It was very rare that there was any doubt as to whether a particular sound was or was not functional in the defined terms, and so was or was not an expression in the language.

This is part of the significance of the functional approach: it provides a criterion for identifying what is language and what is not. It should be noted that this criterion excludes all instances which are interpreted as linguistic practice. When the child is practising speech sounds, or later on when he is practising words, or phrases or other structures, this is not an instance of language in use; it is not a kind of meaning. To say this is merely tantamount to saying that learning a particular system cannot be categorized in terms of the use of that system, and therefore in the present study those utterances which were purely directed towards the learning of the system were omitted from consideration. It happened that Nigel was a child who did very little practice of this kind; some children apparently do a great deal more.

6. Sounds and meanings of Phase I

Figures (1) to (6) show the system of options that Nigel had in his language at each of the six week intervals which I referred to earlier, from 10½ months to 18 months. At 9 months it was possible to identify just two expressions which apparently fulfilled the criteria for being language; they had constant meanings which could be interpreted in terms of the functions listed above, one being interactional, the other personal. These need hardly be regarded as constituting a linguistic system, because in each case there were no alternatives; there was one possible meaning only in the function in question, and no choice.

The set of options that Nigel has at 10½ months, represented in Figure (1), is the earliest that we can significantly characterize as a linguistic system. At 10½ months, Nigel can already use his vocal resources in four out of the six functions that we have identified. In the instrumental function he has one utterance which is a general demand, meaning something like "Give me that" and referring always to some object which is clearly specified in the environment. This contrasts with the specific demand for a favourite object, in this case a toy bird; and it is possible that this represents the one element in the system whose expression is in fact borrowed from the adult language: it may be an imitation of the sound <u>bird</u>. In the regulatory function he has a generalized request, which is always directed to a specific individual, requiring him or her to do something that is again clearly specified in the context, usually by the fact of its having been done immediately before, so that it is equivalent to "Do that again"; this contrasts with an intensified form of the same meaning which carries with it the additional feature of urgency, which is conveyed by the form of the gloss "Do that right now."

In the interactional function, Nigel has a couple of initiating expressions and one response. Of the former, one is a form of greeting, used typically when another person comes newly to his attention, for example someone coming into the room as he wakes up; the utterance directs attention to a particular object, typically a picture, which is then used as the channel for interacting with this other person. The nearest one can get to this in a gloss is something like "How nice to see you, and shall we look at this picture together?", suggesting that the picture becomes the focus of what is in fact a form of interaction that is taking place through language. The other is again an intensified form, an impatient greeting which is not mediated by any joint action; it may be glossed by some such locution as "Nice to see you, and why weren't you here before?" In addition there is a response form, used by Nigel in response to a call or greeting when someone else begins to interact verbally with him. And finally there is a little set of meanings within the personal function, five in all, one of which expresses a state of withdrawal and the others the opposite, a state of participation, involving the expression of some form of pleasure or of interest.

The whole system comprises a set of 12 distinct meanings, and this represents the total semantic potential that the child has at this stage. It is not of course his total semiotic potential, if we define 'semiotic' as the information system that is embodied in the whole of the child's behaviour. But it is his total semantic system —that part of the semiotic that he encodes by means of vocal symbols. It represents what the child can do linguistically, or in other words what he can mean.

We have said that the child's expressions at this stage owe nothing to the adult language. The sounds he makes are not, in general, imitations of the sounds of English words. What then is the origin of these sounds? This is something to which we cannot at this stage hope to give any kind of general answer. But in one or two instances it is possible to derive a hint which throws an interesting sidelight on classical theories of the origins of language. At least one of the expressions in Nigel's earliest linguistic system originates as an imitation by the child of a sound that he heard himself make naturally. In NL 1 the form ġʷʏɪġʷʏɪġʷʏɪ appears, interpreted as having the meaning of withdrawal, and more specifically "I'm sleepy; I want to go to sleep," within the personal function. Now this sound was originally a sound which the child made as an automatic accompaniment to the process of going to sleep. It corresponds to a vocalization of the noise of sucking, perhaps with thumb or bottle in mouth. There came a point when the child transferred the sound into his linguistic system as the expression of one of the meanings in that system. It is interesting to note that shortly afterwards he once again reinterpreted the same sound, this time in the imaginative function as a form of play: at about 13½ months, Nigel would curl up on the floor and produce this sound in a pretence of going to sleep. There are one or two other sounds in Nigel's early systems that could possibly be traced to similar origins.

But there is no obvious source for the great majority of the child's expressions, which appear simply as spontaneous creations of the glossogenic process. As far as the content of Nigel's early systems is concerned, the same observation might be made: the meanings are not, in general, derived from the meanings of the adult language. No doubt, however, the adult language does exert an influence on the child's semantic system from a very early stage, since the child's utterances are interpreted by those around him in terms of their own semantic systems. In other words, whatever the child means, the message which gets across is one which makes sense and is translatable into the terms of the adult language. It is in this interpretation that the child's linguistic efforts are reinforced, and in this way the meanings that the child starts out with gradually come to be adapted to the meanings of the adult language. We have no way at this stage of following through this process in any detail; but it is possible to see in the progression from one stage to the next in Nigel's developing linguistic system how the functional meanings that he expresses gradually become more and more recognizable, as they come to look more and more like the meanings that are encoded in the adult language.

Let us give an example of the way in which the meanings that the child expresses do not correspond exactly to the meanings of the adult language, and the distinctions that the child makes do not correspond to the adult's linguistic distinctions. In NL 3 there is a form yi yi yi yi (high level tone) which Nigel used to respond when he was asked whether he wanted a particular object to be given to him, meaning something like "Yes, I want that." There was also a form a: (high rise-fall) meaning something like "Yes, I want you to do what you have just offered to do," used in response to questions like "Do you want your orange juice now?", or "Shall I put the new record on?" These two meanings represent options within the instrumental function. The first is a response to the offer of some object which is visible, and which may not have been referred to verbally at all. The second is a response to the offer of a service, or of some object which is not itself visible, so that the offer is dependent on the verbalization. The two have quite different intonation patterns; the first is high level, which does not occur systematically in adult English, whereas the second one has something very like the rise-fall tone (tone 5) of the adult language, which gives a sense of "Yes, you've got it: that's what I'm after." The distinction is expressed in the description as a system of options within the instrumental function, a subsystem of the general meaning of *response*; the meaning *response* is in turn contrasted with the meaning of *invitation*, the initiating of a demand by the child himself.

Now any translation of these response items such as "yes, please", or an explanation such as 'positive response to a question,' would be quite inadequate as an inter pretation of these expressions. At this stage, Nigel cannot respond to questions at all—except those in which the answer serves one of the functions that is represented in his linguistic system, either an instrumental function or a regulatory function. In other words, he can respond to questions of the type "Do you want?" or "Shall I?", but not to questions seeking information, such as "Is there?" or "Have you got?". It is not until after 18 months that he begins to be able to respond to questions of this kind, and, when he does, he does it in a very different way. There is nothing in the child's system that corresponds to the general notion of question and answer. These notions depend on a concept of dialogue, of social roles that are defined by the communication process; this concept the child has not yet mastered, and will not master until he is in the process of transition from his own proto-language to the adult language.

Let us take another example. In NL 5 Nigel has two requests for joint action of the type expressed in adult language by let's; these are "Let's go for a walk" and "Let's draw a picture." The first is expressed by a sound of his own invention, a very slow vibration of the vocal cords; the other at first by a sound which is probably an imitation of the word draw and later more often as bow-wow, meaning originally "Let's draw a dog" but now generalized to a sense of "Let's draw a picture." Now these are regulatory in function—they refer to the behaviour of a particular individual; and within the regulatory function they are specific, as contrasted with the general expression meaning "Do that." Further, they are requests for joint action of the "Let's" type, as distinct from requests for action on the part of the other person, such as "Come for lunch". So at this stage Nigel has a little system of just two options within the meaning of "Let's"; and we can see here the earliest manifestations of what gradually develops into an important area of the adult grammatical system, namely the system of *mood*.

7. Beginnings of the transition (phase II)

We shall not attempt to give here a detailed commentary on each stage in the child's development. It is hoped that the representations given in NL 1 to NL 5 are reasonably self-explanatory. They show at each stage the child's meaning potential represented as a network of options deriving from the small set of initial functions that were postulated at the start. They show this meaning potential developing from an initial point at which he is able to express about 12 distinct meanings to one in which the number of meanings has increased to somewhere around 50.

The meanings are represented here in 'systemic' terms; that is to say, as options in the environment of other options. Essentially, language is interpreted in this context not as structure, but as system. Structure refers to the combination of elements one with another: *both* this *and* that; whereas the underlying concept of system is one of choice: *either* this *or* that. Our description represents Nigel's first language as a *semantic* choice, where the systems are systems of meaning; either this meaning or that. Structures are then the mechanisms by which meanings may be expressed; but structure is only one of a set of possible mechanisms, and it is one which is not yet present in the child's system at this stage. This does not prevent us, however, from recognizing that the system he has is a language.

NL 5 represents the final stage in what we may refer to as Phase I of Nigel's language development, the phase in which the child is developing a language of his own. From this point on, he begins the transition into the adult linguistic system. NL 5 is already characterized by the presence of a considerable number of expressions that are taken from the adult language, and are recognizable as words of English; but, more important, it is characterized by the opening up of new functional meanings. The new developments that are taking place can be seen in the sort of exchange that begins to appear in the period round about 16½ months. Here is a typical sequence of events.

Nigel asks [ádᵞdà] "What's that?". The answer is given "that's an egg". The child imitates egg [a͵yì:], repeating the sound a considerable number of times. Shortly afterwards, the child sees the object in question, or a picture of it, and produces the same sound; and after a further interval he begins to use the same sound without the stimulus of the object, but in terms of one of the functions for which he uses language, for example, in the instrumental meaning of "I want an egg." Then, when he starts to engage in dialogue proper, the word turns up in contexts such as the following (end of NL 6, 1; 5½), where the function is no longer obviously interpretable in the earlier terms:

MOTHER: Did you tell Daddy what you had for tea?
NIGEL (to mother, excitedly): aᵞì . . . ȁ . . . aᵞì . . . aᵞì (egg, ooh! egg, egg!) gɔgɫgɔgʷa (cockadoodledoo; = cornflakes, because of picture on packet; also = weathercock on church so, having just returned from walk, continues with inventory of things seen) tìkᵊ (and sticks!)
MOTHER: You didn't have cornflakes for tea!
NIGEL: lɔu (and holes!)
MOTHER: You didn't have sticks and holes for tea!
NIGEL (returning to the subject in hand): dɔuba (and toast).

It might be thought, as a first guess, that the principal incentive for the child to learn the vocabulary of the adult language would be of a pragmatic nature; that he would learn the new words primarily in order to be able to ask for the objects they represented. But NL 6, which shows a very sudden increase in the total number of meanings, to something of the order of 150, includes a considerable number of items that it would be very unlikely to find in a pragmatic context: words such as bubble, and star, and blood, and eyelid and weathercock. If one comes to examine carefully the utterances that the child makes at this stage and the particular contexts in which they occur, it turns out that the majority of those in which the newly acquired vocabulary items figure are not pragmatic in function at all. They occur, rather, in contexts of observation, recall, and prediction.

First, the child uses the new word to comment on the object

as it comes to his attention; for example stick, translated as "I see a stick." Secondly, two or three weeks later, these words come to be used in contexts of recall: not "I see a stick" but "I saw a stick when I was out for a walk." In such instances Nigel often produced long lists of words, for example ("I saw") [kàkàbàbà-bàuwàugɔ́ʔɫgɔ́ʔɫ̀ŋ̀kᵘ̀ŋ̀kᵘlɔùlɔù] cars, buses, dogs, weathercocks, sticks and holes; likewise sticks, holes, stones, trains, balls and buses. Thirdly, after another short interval again of a week or two, the same items appear in contexts of prediction: "I shall see sticks when I go out for a walk," typically said as he was being dressed ready to go out.

What is the function of utterances of this kind? Clearly they are not pragmatic in the sense that utterances of an instrumental or regulatory nature can be said to be pragmatic; but equally clearly they are not meaningless. In terms of the child's semiotic potential at this stage, it seems that their function is a learning function; not in the sense that they contribute to the child's learning of language—they are quite distinct from instances where the child is practising the items in question, instances which we have already rejected from our functional analysis of the system—but in the sense that they contribute to the child's learning about his environment. The language is being used in a function that we might code as *mathetic*.

The origin of this function can be found in the initial set of functions from which we started out. Just as we can regard the *pragmatic* use of the new words as arising directly from the instrumental and regulatory functions, so we can interpret this *mathetic* function as arising primarily from a combination of two others, the personal and the heuristic. It is possible in fact to trace a direct development from some of the earlier meanings which the child had evolved under these headings: expressions of pleasure and interest on the one hand, and on the other hand the demand for the naming of an object, typically a picture, with which the child was already familiar. Contexts of this kind, in which from about NL 4 onwards Nigel would begin to combine the personal and the heuristic in a little series of interchanges, a sort of proto-dialogue, lead gradually and naturally into contexts in which the child is using newly acquired vocabulary for the purpose of categorizing the phenomena of the environment and relating them to his own experience. At this stage, therefore, we can see a process of functional generalization taking place whereby the newly acquired words and structures are put to use either in a context which we are labelling pragmatic, arising from the instrumental and regulatory functions of Phase I, or in a context of the kind that we are calling mathetic, which arises out of the personal and heuristic functions, the interactional function making some contribution to both.

This interpretation is one which we are led to quite naturally from an inspection of the utterances which Nigel was making at this time, utterances such as on the one hand <u>more meat</u>, <u>mend train</u>, <u>come over-there</u>, <u>draw for-me</u>, which are clearly pragmatic in the context, and on the other hand <u>green car</u>, <u>black cat</u>, <u>tiny red light</u>, and <u>bubbles round-and-round</u>, which are equally clearly not in any sense pragmatic but are representations of what the child observes around him. But it happened that Nigel made the distinction between the pragmatic and mathetic function totally explicit in his own expressions, because from this point on, for six months or more, he spoke all pragmatic utterances on a rising tone and all others on a falling tone. The rising tone meant in effect that some form of response was required, a response either in the form of action or, after a time and increasingly throughout this period, a verbal response. The falling tone meant that no response was required, and the utterance was, as it were, self-sufficient. This particular way of encoding the pragmatic/mathetic distinction is of course Nigel's own individual strategy; but it is likely that the opposition itself is the basis of the child's functional system at this stage, since not only is it observable in the child's own use of language, but more significantly it serves as a transition to the functional organization of the adult language. It is the child's way of incorporating the functions into the linguistic system. In this way he arrives ontogenetically at a linguistic system whose major semantic components are in fact based on a functional opposition, that between the ideational and the interpersonal functions which we referred to earlier.

8. Grammar and dialogue

Essentially the pragmatic function of the child's transitional phase, Phase II, is that which leads into the interpersonal component of the adult system, while the mathetic leads into the ideational component. The child learns at this stage that in any use of language he is essentially being either an *observer* or an *intruder*. He is an observer to the extent that the language is serving as the means whereby he encodes his own experience of the phenomena around him, while himself remaining apart. He is an intruder to the extent that he is using language to participate, as a means of action in the context of situation. But whereas at the beginning of Phase II, the child can use language in only one function at a time, being either observer or intruder but not both, by the end of Phase II he has learnt to be both things at once; and this is the essential property of the adult language. In Phase II, which in the case of Nigel begins rather suddenly at stage NL 6 (16½–18 months) and continues until roughly the end of his second year, the child is making the transition from his own proto-language to the adult linguistic system, and this transition involves two fundamental steps.

In the first place, the child has to interpolate a third level in between the content and the expression of his developmental system. The adult language is not a two-level system but a three-level system; it is composed not merely of meanings and sounds, but has another level of coding in between, one which, using folk-linguistic terminology, we may refer to as a level of *wording*. In technical terms, in addition to a semantics and a phonology, he has a level of linguistic form, a lexico-grammar. And the need for the lexicogrammatical level of coding intermediate between meaning and sound arises not merely because of the increased semantic load that the system has to bear, but also because there has to be a means of mapping on to one another meanings deriving from different functional origins. This is achieved by grammatical structure. Grammatical structure is a device which enables the speaker to be both observer and intruder at the same time; it is a form of polyphony in which a number of melodies unfold simultaneously, one semantic 'line' from each of the functional components. With a grammar one is free to mean two things at once.

The second of the two fundamental steps that the child takes in embarking on Phase II, the transition to the adult language, is that of learning to engage in dialogue. Dialogue is, for him, a very new concept. Dialogue involves the adoption of roles which are social roles of a new and special kind, namely those which are defined by language itself. We may refer to these as *communication roles*.

A speaker of the adult language, every time he says anything, is adopting a communication role himself, and at the same time is assigning another role, or a role choice, to the addressee, who, in his turn, has the option of accepting or rejecting the role that is assigned to him. In Phase I, the child has no concept of dialogue or of communication roles; but towards the end of this phase he begins to get the idea that language is itself a form of interaction, and he starts to engage in dialogue. Nigel, at the same time as he was beginning to build a grammar and vocabulary, also took the first steps in dialogue, learning to interact linguistically in a limited number of ways. He learned to respond to an information or 'WH-' type question, one in which the respondent is required to fill in a missing item, such as "What are you eating?". He learned to respond to a command, not only obeying the instruction it contained, but verbalizing the process as he did so. He learned to respond to a statement, not only repeating it but continuing the conversation by adding his own contribution. And finally he learned to initiate dialogue himself, having first of all only one option under this heading, namely the question "What is that?". He could not at this stage ask any other questions, nor could he respond to questions of the confirmation or 'Yes/no' type. But he had clearly internalized the notion that language defines a set of social roles which are to be taken on by the participants in the speech situation; and this is the essential step towards the mastering of the final one in the list of functions that we enumerated at the beginning, namely the informative function.

The use of language to inform is a very late stage in the linguistic development of the child, because it is a function which depends on the recognition that there are functions of language which are solely defined by language itself. All the other functions in the list are extrinsic to language. They are served by and realized through language, but they are not defined by language. They represent the use of language in contexts which exist independently of the linguistic system. But the informative function has no existence independent of language itself. It is an intrinsic function which the child cannot begin to master until he has grasped the principle of dialogue, which means until he has grasped the fundamental nature of the communication process.

Some way on in what we are calling Phase II, Nigel did begin to use language in the informative function; but when he did so he introduced into the system a semantic distinction of his own, another example of a semantic distinction that does not exist in the adult language, between giving information that is already known to the hearer and giving information that is not known. By this stage, Nigel had learnt the grammatical distinction between declarative and interrogative; but he used this distinction not to express the difference between statement and question, since as we have already noted he had at this stage no concept of asking 'Yes/no' questions, but to make a distinction between the two types of information giving. He used the declarative form to give information that he knew was already possessed by the hearer, to represent experience that had been shared by both; and he used the interrogative form to convey information that he knew the hearer did not possess, to refer to an experience which had not been shared between the two. So, for example, if he was building a tower and the tower fell down, he would say to someone who was present and who was taking part with him <u>The tower fell down</u>. But to someone who had not been in the room at the time, and for whom the information was new, he would say <u>Did the tower fall down?</u>. This is a rather useful semantic distinction, and it seems a pity it should be lost in the adult language.

The important point concerning the two major new developments that define the beginning of Phase II, the learning of grammar and the learning of dialogue, is that they take place at the same time. These are the two essential characteristics of the adult linguistic system that are absent from the proto-language that the child creates for himself. It is as if up to a certain point the child was working his own way through the history of the human race, creating a language for himself to serve those needs which exist independently of language and which are an essential feature of human life at all times and in all cultures. Then comes a point when he abandons the phylogenetic trail and, as it were, settles for the language that he hears around him, taking over in one immense stride its two fundamental properties as a system: one, its organization on three levels, with a lexicogrammatical level of wording intermediate between the meaning and the sounding, a level which generates structures which enable him to mean more than one thing at a time; and two, its ability to function as an independent means of human interaction, as a form of social intercourse which generates its own set of roles and role relationships, whose meaning is defined solely by the communication process that language brings about.

These two developments take place more or less simultaneously. They are the crucial features of Phase II, which we have defined as the phase that is transitional between the child's proto-language and his mastery of the adult linguistic system. By the end of Phase II, the child has effectively mastered the linguistic *system* of the adult language. He will spend the rest of his life learning the language itself.

9. Summary

Let us attempt now to summarize the main points so far. We started with the hypothesis that learning the mother tongue consists of mastering certain basic functions of language and in developing a meaning potential in respect of each. The hypothesis was that these functions, namely the instrumental, the regulatory, the interactional, the personal, the heuristic, and the imaginative, represented the developmental functions of language, those in respect of which the child first created a system of meanings; and that some ability to mean in these functions, or in a majority of them, was a necessary and sufficient condition for the learning of the adult language. It is presumed that these functions are universals of human culture, and it is not unreasonable to think of them as the starting point not only for linguistic ontogeny but also for the evolution of the linguistic system.

Within each function the child develops a set of options, a range of alternatives whose meanings are derived from the function in question. The language which the child develops in this way is a simple content-expression system. It contains no grammar and no vocabulary; that is to say, no level of coding intermediate between the semantics and the phonology. It represents a meaning potential, what the very small child can do with this language, together with the resources for expressing the meanings in question. What the child can do at this stage is not a great deal, but it is significant in terms of his own needs. In the case of Nigel we find the system expanding from an initial stage (NL 1) at $10\frac{1}{2}$ months, in which he has 12 choices in meaning at his command, to a stage (NL 5) at $16\frac{1}{2}$ months when the total number of semantic options has reached 50. This is still of course a very slender resource by comparison with what we know as language; but it is worth noting not only that each element in the system is used very frequently —on numerous occasions, not counting repetitions—but also, and more significantly, that some elements are very general in their application. In each function there tends to be one semantically unmarked term, whose meaning is equivalent to that function in its most general scope; for example, "I want that" represents the generalized meaning of language in the instrumental function, where "that" is clearly indicated by the context. This appears to be the origin of what I have called elsewhere the 'good reason' principle in the adult language, a very general and all-pervasive principle whereby, at very many points in the system, the speaker has an

33

option which is unmarked in the sense that it is the option that he selects unless there is good reason for selecting something else. In many of these functions, the child will have one option which he selects as the expression of a general meaning in the absence of any reason for selecting a more specific option within the same function.

In Phase I the child uses the vocal resources of intonation and articulation. He knows from observing linguistic interaction around him that these resources are used by others in meaningful ways. He cannot of course copy the particular sound-meaning correspondences, but he invents a set of his own, using, for example, rise and fall in pitch to express meaning distinctions that exist within his own system. For some time, often perhaps about six or nine months, the child continues to expand the system that he is creating along these lines by adding new semantic contrasts within the existing range of functions; he goes on inventing his own sounds, but comes increasingly to borrow the expressions from the words of the adult language.

There comes a point however at which he moves into a new stage of development, characterized on the one hand by the introduction of a level of vocabulary and structure, and on the other hand by the beginning of dialogue. In Nigel's case this stage began at NL 6, at which the number of distinct meanings rose sharply from 50 to something approaching 150. But, by the same token, it ceases at this point to be possible to interpret the system as a simple inventory of meanings, so that there is no longer much significance to the figure that is obtained in this way. This is because the child is now entering on a new phase of semantic development. The fact that he begins to engage in dialogue, taking on different social roles and assigning these roles to others, means that we can no longer make a simple list of the meanings that the child can express. Furthermore he is developing a semantics that is not only a lexical semantics but also a grammatical semantics, a meaning potential that is organized in sets of options which combine with each other; each choice is by itself very simple, but the combinations form highly complex patterns. The system network that represents the semantics at this stage is no longer a simple taxonomy, as it was before.

The new meanings are incorporated into the child's existing set of functions. There is no discontinuity here in the meanings as there is in the expressions, but rather a continuing development of the potential that is already there. At the same time, however, the very expansion of this potential leads to a development of the child's functional system into a new form: from having been equivalent simply to 'uses of language,' the functions come to be reinterpreted at a more abstract level, through a gradual process whereby they are eventually built into the heart of the linguistic system.

This happens in two stages: first, by the generalization, out of the initial set of developmental functions, of a fundamental distinction between language as doing and language as learning—the pragmatic and the mathetic functions, as we called them; and secondly, by the process of abstraction through which this basic functional opposition is extended from the semantic system into the lexicogrammatical system, so that it becomes the source of the systematic distinction in the adult language between the ideational component, that which expresses the phenomena of the real world, and the interpersonal component, that which expresses the structure of the communication situation. Thus there is a total continuity between the set of functions formulated as part of our initial hypothesis, and the functional organization of the linguistic system that has always been recognized in one form or another in functional theories of language.

There is continuity at the same time on another level, in that the initial functions which language serves for the child evolve at the same time into the types of situation, or contexts of language use. The situation type determines for the adult the particular variety or register he uses, the set of semantic configurations (and the forms of their expression) that can be recognized as typically associated with the abstract properties of the context of situation. We could express this dual continuity another way by saying that, whereas for the very small child in Phase I the concept of *function of language* is synonymous with that of *use of language*, for the adult however the two are distinct; the former refers to what are now incorporated as components of the linguistic system, while the latter refers to the extralinguistic factors determining how the resources of the linguistic system are brought into play. But both *function* and *use* develop in a direct line from their origins in the child's first system of meaning potential.

We have interpreted the linguistic system as essentially a system of meanings, with associated forms and expressions as the realization of these meanings. We have interpreted the learning of language as learning how to mean. At the end of Phase II, which in the case of Nigel was at about $22\frac{1}{2}$ to 24 months, the child has learned how to mean, in the sense that he has mastered the adult linguistic system. He has mastered a system that is multifunctional and multistratal. This system has a massive potential; in fact it is open-ended, in that it can create indefinitely many meanings and indefinitely many sentences and clauses and phrases and words for the expression of these meanings. The child will spend the rest of his life exploring the potential of this system; having learnt how to walk, he can now start going places. Language can now serve him as an effective means of cultural transmission, as a means whereby in the ordinary everyday interaction in which he himself takes part the essential meanings of the culture can be transmitted to him. The culture is itself a semiotic system, a system of meanings or information that is encoded in the behaviour potential of the members, including their verbal potential—that is, their linguistic system. The linguistic system is only one form of the realization of the more general semiotic system which constitutes the culture. But perhaps it is the most important form of realization of it, because it is a prerequisite of most if not all the others. Although there are many aspects of the social semiotic that are not encoded in linguistic forms and expressions, it is likely that most of these draw in some way or other on the system of meanings that constitutes the essence of language.

The child who has learned how to mean has taken the essential step towards the sharing of meanings, which is the distinctive characteristic of social man in his mature state. But in following through any one child's progress we are bound to proceed with caution. Certain of his forward moves no doubt represent universal patterns of human development; others, equally certainly, are his own individual strategy, representing patterns which are no necessary part of the semogenic process. In between these two extremes lies a vast area in which we do not know how much of what we interpret as taking place is to be projected as universal. The steps in Nigel's progression from proto-language to adult language have been mapped out and formulated here in terms which would allow them to be considered as part of a more general hypothesis. But a general hypothesis does not consist solely of statements of universals. It is as much a hypothesis about human variation as about human invariance, and is as much concerned with what is more or less likely as with what is certain. In the last resort it is only the end product that we can be sure is in some sense universal; and we still do not know any too much about that.

3 Learning how to mean

1. Developmental functions: a hypothesis

Seen from a sociolinguistic viewpoint, the learning of the mother tongue appears to comprise three phases of development. The first phase consists in mastering certain basic functions of language, each one having a small range of alternatives, or 'meaning potential', associated with it.

The suggested set of functions in which a child first learns to mean was described in the previous chapter:

Instrumental	'I want'
Regulatory	'do as I tell you'
Interactional	'me and you'
Personal	'here I come'
Heuristic	'tell me why'
Imaginative	'let's pretend'
Informative	'I've got something to tell you'

The hypothesis was that these functions would appear, approximately in the order listed, and in any case with the 'informative' significantly last; that in Phase I, they would be separate from one another, with each expression (and therefore each utterance) having just one function; and that the mastery of all of them—with the possible exception of the last—would be both a necessary and a sufficient condition for the transition to the adult system. It is conceivable that these functions determine the initial development of language in all cultures; if so this would have major implications for our understanding of the evolution of language.

2. The functional interpretation of child language

The criterion adopted for regarding a vocalization by the child as an instance of language was that there must be an observable and constant relation between the content and the expression: that each particular expression must be observed in at least three unambiguous instances, and its content must be interpreted in functional terms. In practice, however, the distinction between random vocalizations and systematic (that is, linguistic) utterances proved to be obvious, and the latter were found to occur with far more than minimal frequency.

This requirement meant that the meaning of what the child was trying to say had to be, in each case, derivable from something that could reasonably be interpreted as a possible function of language—as a context for effective verbal action, whether or not it appeared in the above list. This is what is implied by Leopold's observation that his daughter, at eight months, showed 'the intention of communication, which must be considered the chief criterion of language'. On these criteria, Nigel's vocalizations at 9 months were still pre-linguistic, or just on the threshold of language. At 10½ months, however, he had a language, consisting of a meaning potential in each of four functions. This is what was called NL 1, 'Nigel's Language 1'. (Figure 1).

At this stage, as we have seen, there is no grammar. That is to say, there is no level of linguistic 'form' (syntax, morphology, vocabulary) intermediate between the content and the expression. In stratificational terms, the child has a semology and a phonology but not yet a lexology. Furthermore, the system as a whole owes nothing to the English language (a possible exception being [bø] 'I want my toy bird'). The sounds are spontaneous and, in general, unexplained, although two or three are attested as imitations of natural sounds which the child has heard himself make and then put to systematic use. As has already been pointed out, a phonetic alphabet such as the IPA notation is not very appropriate as a means of representing the child's speech sounds at this stage; it is too specific. What is wanted is a system of notation showing generalized postures and prosodic values.

Rather, it should be said that the expression owes nothing to the English language. As far as the content is concerned, the English language probably has played a part, by virtue of the fact that it embodies meanings such as 'I want that' somewhere in its semantic system, and the adult hearer therefore recognizes and responds to such meanings. It is immaterial whether such meanings are or are not cultural and linguistic universals; what matters is that they are present in the mother tongue.

Nigel's language was studied continuously, and the description of it was recast every 1½ months (figures 1–6). This was the interval that appeared to be optimal: with a longer interval, one might fail to note significant steps in the progression, while, with a shorter one, one would be too much at the mercy of random non-occurrences in the data. Table 1 (p. 147) shows the number of options within each function at each stage from NL 1 (9–10½ months) to NL 5, the end of Phase I (15–16½ months). Those for NL 6, which is considered to be the beginning of Phase II, are added for comparison, although it should be stressed that they are not only less reliable but also, as will emerge from what follows, less significant as an index of the system.

3. Characteristics of Phase I systems

The set of options comprising NL 1 represents what a very small child can do with language—which is quite a lot, in relation to his total behaviour potential. He can use language to satisfy his own material needs, in terms of goods or services (instrumental); to exert control over the behaviour of others (regulatory); to establish and maintain contact with those that matter to him (interactional); and to express his own individuality and self-awareness (personal). Moreover, any one option may have a very considerable range; not only in the sense that it can be used very frequently (on numerous occasions, not counting the repetitions on any one occasion: it is necessary to distinguish 'instances' from 'tokens' at this stage), but also, and more significantly, in the sense that many of the options are very general in their applicability. There is a tendency, we noted, for each function to include an unmarked option, one whose meaning is equivalent to the general meaning of the function in question. For example, in the instrumental function there is one option meaning simply 'I want that', where the object of desire is clear from the context—contrasting with one or more specific options such as 'I want my bird'. There are various modifications of this pattern; for instance, there may be one unmarked term for an initiating context and another for a response ('yes I do want that'). But there is already a principle of unmarked options in meaning; and it seems to resemble the 'good reason' principle, that of 'select this option unless there is a good reason for selecting some other one', that is such a fundamental feature of adult language.

The functions observed in Nigel's Phase I did turn out to be those of the initial hypothesis. This ceases to be true in Phase II; but in one important respect the hypothesis fails already—there is no sign of a developmental progression within the first four functions. As a matter of fact the only two expressions recorded before nine months that fulfil the criteria for language were in the interactional and personal areas. Furthermore, the imaginative function seems to appear before the heuristic, although a reinterpretation of certain elements (the 'problem area' which is referred to in the next paragraph) in the light of Phase II observations suggests that this may be wrong, and that the heuristic function begins to appear at NL 4 ($13\frac{1}{2}$–15 months), at the same time as the imaginative. The two are closely related: the heuristic function is language in the exploration of the objective environment—of the 'non-self' that has been separated off from the self through the development of the personal function—while the imaginative is language used to create an environment of one's own, which may be one of sound or of meaning and which leads eventually into story, song and poetry. Finally, the informative function has not appeared at all. What does emerge as some sort of developmental sequence, in Nigel's case, is (i) that the first four functions listed clearly precede the rest, and (ii) that all others precede the informative. The informative function does not appear until nearly the end of Phase II, round about NL 9 (21–$22\frac{1}{2}$ months); but this was not entirely unexpected, since the use of language to convey information is clearly a derivative function, one which presupposes various special conditions including, for one thing, the concept of dialogue.

The functions themselves, however, emerge with remarkable clarity. Not only did it prove surprisingly easy to apply the general criteria for identifying a vocal act as language (since the learning of a system cannot be regarded as a function of that system, anything interpreted as linguistic practising was left out—as already remarked, Nigel did very little of this); it was possible, throughout NL 1–5, to assign utterances to expressions, expressions to meanings and meanings to functions with relatively little doubt or ambiguity. There was one significant exception to this, a problem area lying at the border of the interactional and the personal functions, which proved extremely difficult to systematize; subsequent interpretation suggest that it was, in fact, the origin of heuristic language, or rather of the generalized 'mathetic' function that is discussed more fully below. Otherwise, although the functions clearly overlap in principle, or at least shade into one another, the value of an element at all levels in the system was usually not difficult to establish.

More important, the fact that the meanings could be derived from functions that were set up on extra-linguistic grounds justifies our regarding these early utterances as expressions of language —a step that is necessary if we are to understand the genesis of language as a whole. Phase II, which corresponds to what has usually, in recent years, been taken as the (unexplained) point of origin of the system, is here regarded as being already transitional, and explained as a reinterpretation of the elementary functions in a more generalized form. Ultimately, these evolve into the abstract functional components of the adult grammatical system; and these components then serve as the medium for the encoding, in grammar, of the original functions in their concrete extensions as what we would call simply 'uses of language'.

PHASE II: THE TRANSITION

4. Vocabulary and structure: vocabulary

The transition to the adult system begins, with Nigel, at NL 6 (16½–18 months). This phase is characterized by two main features: (i) a shift in the functional orientation, which is described below, and (ii) major and very rapid advances in vocabulary, in structure, and in dialogue.

Vocabulary and structure are in principle the same thing. What emerges at this point is a grammar, in the traditional sense of this term in which it refers to the level of linguistic 'form'—strictly speaking, a lexicogrammar. This is a system intermediate between the content and the expression, and it is the distinguishing characteristic of human, adult language. The options in the grammatical system are realized as structure and vocabulary, with vocabulary, as a rule, expressing the more specific choices.

NL 6 has some 80–100 new meanings, and, for the first time, the majority of the meanings are expressed by means of lexical items—the expressions are English words. In the first instance these are used holophrastically, which in the present context is defined in functional terms: the lexical item forms, by itself, an utterance that is functionally independent and complete. With

Nigel, this did not continue very long; he happened to be one of those children who hardly go through a 'holophrastic stage', for whom the holophrase is merely the limiting case of a linguistic structure. In any case the holophrase is, in itself, of little importance; but it serves to signal the very crucial step whereby the child introduces words—that is, a vocabulary—into his linguistic system.

Why does the child learn words? Do they fit into and enrich the existing functional pattern, or are they demanded by the opening up of new functional possibilities? The answer seems to be, not unexpectedly, both.

Many of the words that are learnt first are called for by existing functions. Of these the majority, in Nigel's case, are at first restricted to one function only; e.g. cat means only 'hullo, cat!' (interactional), syrup means only 'I want my syrup' (instrumental). A few then begin to appear in more than one function, but at different times; e.g., hole means now 'make a hole' (instrumental), now 'I want to (go out for a walk and) put things in holes' (regulatory) and now 'look, there's a hole' (personal-heuristic; see below). Just once or twice, we find a combination of two functions in a single instance; e.g. cake meaning 'look, there's a cake —and I want some!' This last is very striking when it first occurs. With the adult, all utterances are plurifunctional; but for a child the ability to mean two things at once marks a great advance.

Thus, as far as the existing functions are concerned, the learning of vocabulary (i) engenders new meanings within these functions and (ii) allows for the functions to be combined. The latter of these developments will come to impose definite requirements on the nature of linguistic structure, since the principal role of structure, in grammar, is that of 'mapping' different functional meanings one on to another. That is to say, the structures that the child develops have to be such that they allow him—as the structures of the adult language do—to mean more than one thing at a time.

However, many of the new words—the majority in Nigel's case—do not fit into the earlier functional pattern. In the first place, they have clearly not been learnt for pragmatic contexts. Indeed many of them are not particularly appropriate to the instrumental or regulatory functions, e.g. bubble, toe, star, hot, weathercock; and even those that are do not appear in these functions until later on—the words dog and bus, for example, although perfectly well understood as also referring to certain toys, are not used to ask for those toys, or in any other pragmatic sense.

It might be surmised, then, that the impetus to the learning of new words would come from the emergence of the informative function, from the child's desire to use language for conveying information. But this is not so. At 18 months Nigel has no conception of language as a means of communicating an experience to someone who has not shared that experience with him; it is only much later that he internalizes the fact that language can be used in this way. A further possibility might be that the child is simply practising, using new words just in order to learn them. This also must be rejected, if it implies that the child is learning language in order to learn language; he cannot seriously be thought to be storing up verbal wealth for future uses he as yet knows nothing about. But the notion of learning is the relevant one, provided it is interpreted as learning in general, not simply the learning of language. For Nigel, the main functional impetus behind the move into the lexical mode is, very distinctly, that of learning about his environment. Most of the new vocabulary is used, at first, solely in the context of observation and recall: 'I see/hear . . .', including 'I saw/heard . . .'.

In terms of the developmental functions, this appears to be a blend of the personal and the heuristic, resulting from some such process as the following. First, the self is separated from the 'non-self' (the environment). Second, a meaning potential arises in respect of each: the self is represented by personal reactions, e.g. 'pleasure', and the environment by attention to external phenomena, e.g. 'look!'. Third, new meanings arise through the combination of the two: both involvement with, and reaction to, features of the environment, e.g. 'look, that's interesting!'. Fourth, the child develops a semantics for the interpretation and structuring of the environment in terms of his own experience.

Hence the new words function mainly as a means of categorizing observed phenomena, and provide the earliest instance of the use of language as a means of learning. Many of them represent items having properties that are difficult to assimilate to experience, typically movement (e.g. dog bee train bubble) and visual or auditory prominence (e.g. tower light bus drill); while others are simply phenomena that are central to the child's personal explorations—in Nigel's case, particularly things in pictures. The child is constructing a heuristic hypothesis about the environment, in the form of an experiential semantic system whose meanings are realized through words and structures, and which is used in contexts of observations and recall—and before long also of prediction.

This learning function of language appears to arise as a synthesis of the two principal non-pragmatic Phase I functions: the personal, which is the self-oriented one, and the heuristic, which is other-oriented. Nigel's earliest instances, at the beginning of Phase II, are markedly other-oriented; but this function soon becomes a means of exploring the self as well, and so takes up, on a higher level, the meaning of the original Phase I 'personal' function. We can trace the history of this mathetic function of language in Nigel's case from the very beginning; it is of interest not only because it shows the steps whereby language came to be a means of learning but also because it reveals what was, for Nigel, the primary mode of entry into grammar.

Prominent in NL 1 is an interactional option in which some pleasurable experience, usually a picture, is used as the channel for contact with another person: [dɔ] &c., glossed as 'nice to see you, and shall we look at this together?'. In NL 2, this apparently splits into two meanings, though still with considerable overlap: one having an interactional emphasis, [dɔ], [èya] &c., 'nice to see you (and look at this!)', the other personal, [dɔ], [dɛ̀ə] &c., 'that's nice', reacting to a picture or bright object and not requiring the presence of a second participant. By NL 3, the former has become simply a greeting, and the expression for it is replaced, in NL 4, by hullo [ālóuwa], alongside which appear individualized expressions of greeting <u>Mummy</u>, <u>Daddy</u>, <u>Anna</u>. The latter remains as an expression of personal interest; but meanwhile a third form arises at the intersection of the two, [ādà], [adādādà] &c., which represents the earliest type of *linguistic* interaction, glossed as 'look at this!—now you say its name'—used only where the object is familiar and the name already (receptively) known. In NL 5, this naming request specializes out and becomes the form of demand for a new name, [ædȳdà] 'what's that?'; and this is used constantly as a heuristic device. Meanwhile, alongside the general expression of personal interest there have appeared a few specific variants, 'look that's a . . .', which are expressed by English words. At first these occur only in familiar contexts, again typically pictures; but in NL 6 they come to be used in the categorization of new experience, in the form of observation and recall: 'I see a . . .', 'I saw a . . .'. Then, within a very short time (less than one month), and still largely in this same mathetic function, the vocabulary begins to be backed up by structures. We can thus follow through, with Nigel, the process whereby the use of names to record and comment on what is observed, which is a universal feature of child language at a certain stage, arises out of meanings and functions that already existed for the child before any vocabulary had been learnt at all.

5. Vocabulary and structure: structure

With Nigel, the structural explosion followed very closely on the lexical one. That it is part of the same general process, the development of a lexicogrammatical stratum intermediate between the content and the expression, is shown, however, not so much by the shortness of this interval—which with some children is much longer—but by the fact that both vocabulary and structure first appear in the same functional contexts. All that was said, in functional terms, about the learning of vocabulary could apply to structure also.

Despite a commonly held belief to the contrary, the speech which the child hears around him is, in the typical instance, coherent, well-formed and contextually relevant. In interaction with adults he is not, in general, surrounded by intellectual discourse, with its backtracking, anacolutha, high lexical density and hesitant planning; but by the fluent, smoothly grammatical and richly structured utterances of informal everyday conversation. He has abundant evidence with which to construct the grammatical system of his language. What he hears from other children, naturally, is different—but it is different in ways which serve his as a guide for his own efforts. (This is not, of course, an argument against the nativist hypothesis. But it is an argument against the *necessity* of an interpretation in nativist terms.)

The origin and early development of structure is not the main concern here; it will be touched upon here only insofar as it relates to the functional perspective. At the outset of Phase II, Nigel displayed two types of proto-structure, or rather two variants of the same type: a specific expression, within a certain function, combined either (i) with a gesture or (ii) with a general expression from the same function. Examples: [dà:bi] Dvořak + beating time (music gesture), 'I want the Dvořak record on' (instrumental function); [ndà] star + shaking head (negation gesture), 'I can't see the star' (personal); [ὲ lɔu] command + hole, 'make a hole' (regulatory); [ὺ æyì] excitement + egg, 'ooh, an egg!' (personal). Shortly after this came word strings; these were of two words only, e.g. [bʌbu nɔumɔ] bubble, no more 'the bubbles have gone away', except when in lists, when there might be as many as six, e.g. stick, hole, stone, train, ball, bus 'I saw sticks, &c.'. Here each word still has its own independent (falling) tone contour. The first 'true' structure, in the sense of a string of words on a single tone contour, appeared at 19 months, just four weeks after the first major excursion into vocabulary; and within two more weeks various types of structure were being produced, as in the following sets of examples:

(1) mummy come, more meat, butter on, squeeze orange, mend train, help juice ('help me with the juice'), come over-there, now room ('now let's go to the room'), star for-you ('make a star for me'), more meat please

(2) green car, two book ('two books'), mummy book ('mummy's book'), bee flower ('there's a bee on the flower'), bubble round-round ('the bubbles are going round and round'), tiny red light, two fast train

These structures fall into two distinct groups, on functional criteria. Those under (1) are 'pragmatic', and correspond to the instrumental and regulatory functions of Phase I; while those of (2) are what we have called 'mathetic', deriving from the personal-heuristic functions.

Quite unexpectedly, this binary grouping was made fully explicit by Nigel himself, when within the same two-week period (the end of NL 7, 19 to 19½ months) he introduced an entirely new distinction into his speech, that between falling and rising tone. From this point on, all pragmatic utterances were spoken on a rising tone and all non-pragmatic (mathetic) ones on a falling tone. The distinction was fully systematic, and was maintained intact for some months; it provided a striking corroboration of the significance of pragmatic/mathetic as a major functional opposition. If Nigel is at all typical, this opposition (though not, of course, Nigel's particular form of realization of it) seems to be fundamental to the transition to Phase III, the adult system; we shall return to it below. Here it is relevant because it enables us to see the development of structure in Phase II as an integral part of the total language-learning process.

What is the relation of linguistic structure to the functions of language? Let us take the examples, from Nigel at the beginning of Phase II (NL 7, 18–19½ months), of more meat, two book and green car. All three seem at first sight to display an identical structure, whether this is stated in child-oriented terms, e.g. Pivot + Open, or in adult-oriented terms, e.g. Modifier + Head. But

46

more meat occurs only in a pragmatic function, while the other two occur only in a mathetic function. Moreover this is a general pattern; we find more omelet, more bread &c. all likewise pragmatic only, and two train, mummy book ('mummy's book'), green peg, red car &c. all mathetic only. It is this functional specialization which relates these structures to the earlier stage of language learning. By a subsequent step, they become functionally derestricted, so that the structure represented by more meat becomes compatible with the mathetic sense 'look there's some . . .', and that of green car with the pragmatic sense of 'I want the . . .'. At first, however, each structure is tied exclusively to just one function or the other.

The structural analysis of more meat might be 'Request +Object of desire', relating it to the instrumental function from which it derives. The elements of the structure are pragmatic not experiential ones. By contrast, green car may be analyzed in experiential terms, as perhaps 'Visual property+Object observed'. In terms of the discussion in Chapter 1, this interpretation of structure is child-oriented semantic: semantic in order to relate it to function, child-oriented to show the part it plays developmentally, which is obscured if we assume from the start a final outcome in the shape of a structure of the adult language. Exactly how a structure such as that represented by more meat, initially pragmatic, comes later to take on a non-pragmatic function, first in alternation and then in combination with the pragmatic, is an interesting and difficult question; presumably in this instance the request element more comes to be reinterpreted experientially as a comparative quantifier (in Nigel's case, via the aspectual sense of 'I want (you) to go on . . . ing', e.g. more play rao 'I want us to go on playing lions'); while the request function is generalized and taken over by the modal system in the grammar (in Nigel's case, via the systematic use of the rising tone). We have chosen here what is probably a rather simple example; but the point is a general one. In the beginning, all Nigel's structures, like his vocabulary, are functionally specific; they are either pragmatic (set (1) above), or mathetic (set (2)). Only after an interval are they transferred to the other function; and this takes place, not by a shift out of one box into another, but rather by a recasting of the concept of 'function' on to a more abstract plane so that all expressions become, in effect, plurifunctional.

Herein lies the essential unity of structure and vocabulary.

Words and structures, or rather 'words-and-structures', i.e. lexicogrammatical units, are the expression of options at a new level appearing in the child's linguistic system intermediate between meaning and sound. This is the stratum of linguistic form, or grammar; and it appears that grammar develops, with the child, as the means of incorporating the functional potential into the heart of the linguistic system. It allows for meanings which derive from different functions to be encoded together, as integrated structures, so that every expression becomes, in principle, functionally complex. Grammar makes it possible to mean more than one thing at a time.

6. Dialogue

The early development of the grammatical system has been fairly thoroughly explored. What has been much less explored, though of no less fundamental importance, is how the child learns dialogue.

Nigel learnt to engage in dialogue at the same time as he started to learn vocabulary, towards the end of NL 6 (just before 18 months); and dialogue could serve as well as vocabulary to mark the beginning of his Phase II. There was some 'proto-dialogue' in Phase I: at NL 2, Nigel had three specific responses, to calls, greetings and gifts, and by NL 5 he could answer questions of the type 'do you want . . .?', 'shall I . . .?', i.e. those where the answers required were instrumental, regulatory or interactional in function. But he could not initiate dialogue; nor could he give responses of a purely linguistic kind. He could not, in other words, respond to utterances where the response would have lain outside his functional potential. He could express the meanings 'yes' and 'no' in the senses of 'yes I want that', 'no I don't want that' (instrumental), or 'yes do that', 'no don't do that' (regulatory). But he had no general polarity (positive/negative) system; nor could he respond to any question seeking information, such as 'did you see a car?' or 'what did you see?'

Dialogue can be viewed as, essentially, the adoption and assignment of roles. The roles in question are social roles, but social roles of a special kind: they exist only in and through language, as roles in the communication process—speaker, addressee, respondent, questioner, persuader and the like. But they are of general significance developmentally, since they serve both as a channel and as a model for social interaction. Whenever someone speaks, he normally takes on the role of addresser ('I'm talking to you'),

48

and assigns the role of listener ('attend!'). In dialogue, however, these roles have to be made more specific: not merely 'I'm talking to you' but, for example, 'I am demanding information, and you are to respond by supplying it'. Dialogue involves purely linguistic forms of personal interaction; at the same time, it exemplifies the general principle whereby people adopt roles, assign them, and accept or reject those that are assigned to them.

The mysteries of dialogue were unravelled by Nigel in the two-week period at the opening of NL 7 ($18-18\frac{1}{2}$ months). At the end of this time he could:

(1) respond to a WH-question (provided the answer was already known to the questioner), e.g. 'What are you eating?' Nigel: banana.

(2) respond to a command, e.g. 'Take the toothpaste to Daddy and go and get your bib'. Nigel does so, saying: daddy . . . noddy . . . train, i.e. 'Daddy, (give) noddy (toothpaste to him, and go and get your bib with the) train (on it)'.

(3) respond to a statement, e.g. 'You went on a train yesterday'. Nigel signals attention, by repeating, and continues the conversation: train . . . byebye, i.e. 'yes, I went on a train, and then (when I got off) the train went away'.

(4) respond to a response, e.g. Nigel: gravel. Response: 'Yes, you had some gravel in your hand'. Nigel: ooh, i.e. 'it hurt me'.

(5) initiate dialogue, e.g. Nigel: what's that? Response: 'That's butter'. Nigel repeats: butter.

The question 'what's that?' is, however, his only option for initiating dialogue at this stage. Apart from this, it is outside his functional potential to demand a linguistic response: he cannot yet assign specific communication roles. But he has gone some way in being able to accept those that are assigned to him. As long as the child's responses are limited to exchanges such as these:

('Nigel!') Nigel: [ə̀] 'yes I'm here'

('Do you want some cheese?') Nigel: [nɔ̀] 'no I don't want it'

('Shall I put the lorry in the box for you?') Nigel: [à] 'yes do'

he is simply using language in its original extralinguistic functions; this is not yet true dialogue. The ability to respond to a WH-question, however, is a significant innovation; the child has mastered the principle of the purely communicative functions of language, and is beginning to take on roles that are defined by language itself. (Nigel cannot at this stage respond explicitly to a yes/no question, although he sometimes does so by implication, e.g. 'Are you going shopping?' Nigel: bread . . . egg. i.e. 'I'm going to buy bread and eggs'.) This is the first step towards the 'informative' use of language, which is late in appearing precisely because it is language in a function that is solely defined by language. Imparting information that is not already known, obvious as it may seem to the adult, is, as suggested earlier, a complex and difficult notion.

Once the child can engage in dialogue, new possibilities arise in relation to the functions he has already mastered: the elaboration of existing options, persistence and change in functional 'tactics' and so on. Dialogue also plays an essential part in the development of the generalized mathetic function, not only making it possible for the child to ask for new names but also allowing for systematic exploration of the environment and extended patterns of verbal recall. But no less important than this is the role of dialogue in anticipating and leading into Phase III, the mastery of the adult system. Through its embodiment of linguistic role-playing, dialogue opens the way to the options of mood (declarative, interrogative &c.), and thus to the entire interpersonal component in the language system. This is the component whereby the speaker intrudes or, as it were, builds himself into the linguistic structure, expressing his relations with other participants, his attitudes and judgments, his commitments, desires and the like. Thus in the course of Phase II, with the help of an increasing amount of imitative, role-playing speech—and also of sheer argument, which plays an essential part—the child learns to participate linguistically, and to intrude his own angle, his individuality and his personal involvement into the linguistic structure. In this way language becomes for him an effective channel of social learning, a means of participating in and receiving the culture. Meanings are expressed as verbal interaction in social contexts; this is the essential condition for the transmission of culture, and makes it possible for certain types of context to play a critical part in the socialization process.

Phase II is thus characterized by two major advances towards the adult linguistic system. On the one hand, the child adds a level of linguistic form (a grammar and vocabulary) intermediate between the content and the expression, so developing the basic tri-stratal organization of the adult language. The grammar is a system of potential, a network of options that is capable of 're-ceiving' from the content level and 'transmitting' to the expression. (And the other way round. Relatively little is yet known about the processes whereby the child develops his understanding of what is said to and around him; but it is likely that the crucial step here too is the development of this third, intermediate level in his own linguistic coding system.) In this way, the grammar forms structures, accepting options from various functionally distinct content systems and interpreting these into integrated structural patterns. It is a nexus of systems and structures, as these were defined by Firth.

On the other hand, the child learns dialogue; he learns to adopt, accept and assign linguistic roles, and thus to measure linguistic success in linguistic terms. From now on, success consists no longer simply in obtaining the desired material object or piece of behaviour, but rather in playing one's part; in freely accepting the roles that one is assigned, and getting others to accept those that one has assigned to them.

Phase II can be said to end when the child has mastered the *principles* of grammar and of dialogue, and thus effectively completed the transition to the adult language *system*. He is still, of course, only just beginning his mastery of the adult *language*. But Phase II is transitional also in the functional sense, in that the child is moving from the original set of discrete developmental functions, where 'function' equals 'use', through an intermediate stage leading to the more abstract concept of 'function' that lies at the heart of the adult language. Naturally the two aspects of the transition, the functional and the systemic, are closely interconnected; they are the two sides of the developmental process. The development of the functions, however, is significant for interpreting the development of the system—in the sense that language evolves in the way it does because of what it has to do. In the final section of this chapter, we will sketch out in tentative fashion the nature of the child's functional progression into the adult language.

PHASE III: INTO LANGUAGE

7. Functions of the adult system

Can we relate the 'function' of Phase I, where it refers to a set of simple, unintegrated *uses* of language, instrumental, regulatory and so on, to 'function' in the sense of the highly abstract, integrated networks of relations that make up the adult language system?

The answer will depend on our interpretation of 'function' in the adult language. Functional theories of language have attempted, as a rule, not so much to explain the nature of language in functional terms, as to explain types of language use; their points of departure have been, for example, ethnographic (Malinowski), psychological (Bühler), ethological (Morris), or educational (Britton). But although the categories and terminologies differ, all of these incorporate in some form or other a basic distinction between an ideational (representational, referential, cognitive) and an interpersonal (expressive-conative, social, evocative) function of language.

If we now adapt this functional perspective to a consideration of the nature of language itself, we find that the adult linguistic system is in fact founded on a functional plurality. As we saw, it is structured around this two-way distinction of ideational and interpersonal. The grammar of an adult language is a tripartite network of options, deriving from these two basic functions together with a third, that of creating text—the textual or, we could equally well say, 'textural' function of language. This last is not treated in most functional theories because it is intrinsic to language; it is an enabling function, providing the conditions whereby the other functions can effectively be served. The textual function arises out of the very nature of language, and we need not therefore look for its independent origin in the developmental process. The question then becomes: how does the child progress from the functional pattern of his Phase I linguistic system to the ideational/interpersonal system which is at the foundation of the adult language?

This is the point at which Nigel provided an interesting and unexpected clue. Like all children, apparently, he had made systematic use of intonation from the start, all his expressions being characterized by particular pitch contours: typically, varieties of falling tone, though with some exceptions—all personal names, for example, were high level. Early in Phase II, Nigel introduced within one week (NL 7, $19\frac{1}{4}$–$19\frac{1}{2}$ months) a systematic opposition between rising and falling tone; this he maintained throughout the remainder of Phase II with complete consistency. Expressed in Phase I terms, the rising tone was used on all utterances that were instrumental or regulatory in function, the falling tone on all those that were personal or heuristic, while in the interactional function he used both tones but with a contrast between them. We can generalize this distinction by saying that Nigel used the rising tone for utterances demanding a response, and the falling tone for the others. The few exceptions were themselves systematic. For example, demands for music had, as expected, a rising tone—unless they were accompanied by the music gesture, in which case the tone was falling; this shows that the gesture was an alternative realization of the option 'request for music', and that the falling tone is to be regarded as the unmarked term in the system. The important point to note here is that Nigel is *not* using intonation as it is used in adult English, since the contrasts in meaning that are expressed by intonation in English are still outside his functional potential. He is adapting the elementary opposition between rising and falling, which he knows to be significant, to a functional system that is within his own limitations—and one which, as it happens, is perfectly transitional between Phase I and Phase III. This is the distinction that was referred to earlier, between the pragmatic function, or language as doing, Nigel's rising tone, and the mathetic function, or language as learning, Nigel's falling tone. The one aspect that lies outside this system is the imaginative or play function of language, which at this stage takes the form of chants and jingles with special intonation patterns of their own.

This distinction between two broad generalized types of language use, the mathetic and the pragmatic, that Nigel expresses by means of the contrast between falling and rising tone, turns out to be the one that leads directly in to the abstract functional distinction of ideational and interpersonal that lies at the heart of the adult linguistic system. In order to reach Phase III, the child has to develop two major zones of meaning potential, one ideational, concerned with the representation of experience, the other interpersonal, concerned with the communication process as a form and as a channel of social action. These are clearly marked out in the grammar of the adult language. It seems likely that the ideational component of meaning arises, in general, from the use of language to learn, while the interpersonal arises from the use of language to act. The fact that Nigel made the distinction between the mathetic and the pragmatic fully explicit by means of intonation was, of course, merely his own route through Phase II; it is not to be expected that this distinction will be expressed in the same way by other children, or even that it will necessarily be made explicit at all. But for Nigel this was a major step in his development of a grammatical system, as he progressed from the simple duality of content and expression that is characteristic of Phase I.

It is not to be thought that Phase II 'mathetic' is *synonymous* with ideational, or 'pragmatic' with interpersonal. Pragmatic and mathetic are generalized functional categories of the content, in the developmental system of the child, in which every utterance is, in principle, *either* one *or* the other. Ideational and interpersonal are abstract functional components of the lexico-grammar, in the developed, tristratal system of the adult; here every utterance is, in principle, *both* one *and* the other at the same time. What changes is the concept of 'function'; and from this point of view, Phase II is the developmental process whereby 'function' becomes distinct from 'use'. In other words, the notion 'function of language' splits into two distinct notions, that of 'use of language' and that of 'component of the linguistic system'. We shall try to summarize this process, together with other aspects of the entry into Phase III, in the final sections of this chapter (sections 8–9). A further step in the interpretation will be suggested in Chapter 4.

8. Summary

(1) The origins of language development can be interpreted as the learning of a set of functions, each with its associated 'meaning potential'. The system is a functional one, in which function is identical with use: each utterance has one function only, and the meanings are such as 'give me that', 'I'm interested', 'let's be together'. The initial functions are instrumental, regulatory, interactional and personal; these are then followed by the heuristic and the imaginative. Each item in the language is a simple content-expression pair; there is no level of linguistic 'form' (no grammar).

(2) At a certain stage, the child begins to use language in a 'mathetic' function, for the purpose of learning. This arises as a generalization from the personal and the heuristic; language in the identification of the self and, as a corollary, in the exploration of the non-self. This function is realized through verbal observation and recall (and, later, prediction). It generates a range of new meanings for which the child needs resources of vocabulary (e.g. names of objects and processes) and of structure (e.g. class and property, process and participant).

(3) Simultaneously there appears to take place a general-

ization of the remaining functions under a 'pragmatic' rubric which includes the use of language both to satisfy one's own needs and to control and interact with others, subsuming what is sometimes called 'manipulative' language. This also generates new meanings, for which other structures are required (e.g. Request plus Object of desire), and also other lexical items. With Nigel, however, only a minority of words was first learnt in this function, perhaps because often the specific meaning is recoverable from the situation (e.g. 'I want that').

(4) The grouping into mathetic and pragmatic functions appeared, with Nigel, as the dominant characteristic of Phase II, the transitional phase. The distinction is that between language as learning and language as doing; between *separating* the self from the environment, thus identifying the one and interpreting the other, and *interacting* with the environment so as to intrude on the things and people in it, manipulating them and expressing attitudes towards them. With Nigel, nearly all words and structures were first used to express meanings in either one or the other of these two functions but not in both; after an interval, the resources that had been mastered in the one function were then transferred to the other. But, at the same time, all utterances were becoming plurifunctional; see 10 below.

(5) In its inception, the mathetic/pragmatic distinction corresponds to one of 'response required' (pragmatic) versus 'response not required' (mathetic). This probably accounts for the remarkably explicit form given to this distinction by Nigel, who used rising tone to express the pragmatic meaning and falling tone for the mathetic. The question whether the mathetic/pragmatic distinction represents a general Phase II strategy must be left open at this stage; the use of intonation to express the distinction is, of course, Nigel's own idea.

(6) As far as the linguistic system is concerned, Phase II consists in learning grammar; that is, in introducing into the system a level of linguistic form, interposed between content and expression and made up of sets of options realized as structure and vocabulary. The need for a lexico-grammar arises out of the pragmatic and the mathetic functions; the latter (whether or not it is of greater significance for cognitive development) seems to provide the main initial impetus for the learning of vocabulary. The introduction of grammatical structure makes it possible, however, to combine both functions in one utterance.

(7) At the same time as learning grammar, the child also learns

55

dialogue. This is the other major step characterizing Phase II. Here the main impetus probably comes from the pragmatic functions, with their emphasis on involvement. With dialogue, the child acquires a potential for adopting and assigning linguistic roles, which in turn calls for further resources in the grammar (e.g. a set of options in mood—declarative, interrogative and so on—and the structures which are used to realize them).

Note: It is the system of mood that is eventually going to determine the patterns of rising and falling tone. How does Nigel adapt this to his own interpretation of rise and fall? At this stage, he has no system of mood other than that which is expressed by his his own use of the distinction of rise and fall, i.e. the pragmatic/mathetic system; the demand for a new name, [ædȳdà] 'what's that?', cannot really be regarded as an interrogative—it is true that it always has a falling tone, but this is not because it is a WH-question (he has no WH-question at this stage), but because it has a mathetic function. When he does learn the WH-question form where + personal name, this at first has either tone, with (it seems) a difference in meaning between the two; but subsequently this and all other WH-questions take on the rising tone, presumably on the grounds that an answer is a form of response (even though a purely linguistic one), and that demanding an answer is therefore a type of pragmatic function. Later still he learns the yes/no interrogative form; but this is not used for asking questions at all—it is used solely as the realization of the informative function, to communicate experience not shared by the hearer, e.g. did you fall down 'I want you to know that I fell down—you didn't see the event', contrasting with you fell down 'I fell down—as you saw'.

(8) Functionally speaking, the grammar of the adult language comprises the two major components (i) ideational, embodying the speaker's experience and interpretation of the world that is around him and inside him, and (ii) interpersonal, embodying his own involvement in the speech situation—his roles, attitudes, wishes, judgments and the like. To express this another way, the linguistic system has evolved so as to serve, for the speaker, on the one hand the 'observer' function and on the other hand the 'intruder' function. These two 'meta-functions', together with a third, the 'textual' function, are incorporated in the system of the adult language as distinct sets of options, each having strong internal but weak external constraints (i.e. a choice within one function affects other choices within the same function but not, in general, those outside it). Each set of options is realized through

distinct structures which are mapped on to one another in the production of utterances.

(9) It follows that, in Phase III (the adult system), 'function' is no longer synonymous with 'use'. The adult has indefinitely many uses of language; but the typical utterance of the adult language, whatever its use, has both an ideational and an interpersonal component of meaning. For example, every main clause embodies selections—and therefore is structured—simultaneously in transitivity (ideational) and in mood (interpersonal).

(10) It appears, then, that the 'meta-functions' of the Phase III grammatical system arise, indirectly but unmistakably, out of the primary uses of language that the child develops in Phase I. On the evidence of Nigel, the transition takes place by a process of generalization from these primary functions, which yields the two broad function types of pragmatic and mathetic. The pragmatic is oriented towards meanings such as 'I want', 'will you?', 'may I?', 'let's'; so it provides the context for the interpersonal systems of the grammar, typically those of mood, modality, person, attitude and the like. The mathetic is oriented towards experiential meanings, and so provides the context for ideational systems such as those of transitivity (the grammar of processes), time and place, qualifying and quantifying, and so on.

(11) Hence the child's Phase I functional system, which is a system of the *content* in a 'content, expression' language, evolves along the familiar lines of generalization followed by abstraction, into the Phase III (adult) functional system, which is a system of the *form* in a 'content, form, expression' language. The concept of function has itself evolved in the process (cf. Figure 7, p. 158). In terms of Hjelmslev's theory of language, the functional basis of language has shifted from the 'content substance' (in a system having no level of form) into the 'content form'. The child, at Phase II, makes the crucial discovery that, with language, he can both observe and interact with the environment at the same time; this is the significance of Nigel's 'that's cake—and I want some!'. By the time he enters Phase III the child has a great many 'uses' of language; but all of them are actualized through the medium of the ideational and the interpersonal 'functions'; in other words, through his twofold meaning potential as observer and as intruder.

(12) Meanwhile therefore the original Phase I functions have not just disappeared. It is these that have become the uses of language—or rather, they have become the generalized social

contexts of language use. In addition to those that seem to have been the key to the transition process, two others had been postulated, the imaginative and the informative. The imaginative, or play, function of language is present already in Phase I; by the end of Phase II, the child is playing not only with sounds but with forms and meanings as well, reciting, distorting and inventing rhymes, routines and stories. Eventually—but not until well into Phase II—he adds the informative function, the use of language to communicate experience to someone who did not share it with him; this is a highly complex function, since it is one that is solely defined by language itself.

The imaginative and informative functions call for the narrative mode (within the ideational component) as distinct from simple observation and recall. This in turn requires discourse, i.e. text which is structured so as to be relevant not only to the situation but also to the verbal context, to what is said before and after. What we referred to as the 'textual' component in the linguistic system can be seen developing, with Nigel, in response to the needs of dialogue and of narrative.

At the same time, language still serves, for the child, the uncomplicated functions for which he first learnt it. Only, their scope is now immeasurably enlarged, in breadth and in depth: in other words in the meaning potential that is associated with each.

9. Prospect

By the end of Phase II, the child has entered the adult language. He has built up a system that is multistratal (content, form, expression) and multifunctional (ideational, interpersonal, textual). From this point on, he is adding to what he already has. He has learnt *how* to mean; his language development now consists in extending the range of his meaning potential to broader cultural horizons.

In order to follow this process further, we shall have to go outside the linguistic system and into the culture. The child's uses of language are interpretable as generalized situation types; the meanings that he can express are referable to specific social contexts, and at least in some instances may be approached through a context-specific semantic analysis such as is exemplified in Geoffrey Turner's studies of parental speech behaviour.

Bernstein has shown that certain types of social context are critical to the process of cultural transmission; the language of these contexts plays a crucial part in the child's socialization. Now, as we have seen, all language behaviour, including that which characterizes these critical contexts, is mediated through the basic functions of language, the observer function and the intruder function; and the meanings that are expressed are linked, in this way, to what Malinowski called the 'context of situation'. But because these functions are not simply aspects of the use of language, but are part of—indeed, are the heart of—the linguistic system, the specific meanings expressed are at the same time instances of general semantic categories, and hence are interpreted in the 'context of culture' (to use another of Malinowski's concepts).

What is the significance of this for the child? The significance is that, because of the functional basis of language, the particular, concrete meanings that are expressed in typical everyday situations become, for him, the primary source for *building up* the context of culture. By the time he reaches Phase III, each instance of 'I want' or 'may I?' or 'let me take part' or 'what's going on?' is encoded in words and structures which serve in some measure to categorize the social order and the child's own part in it. So it happens that the child's own early uses of language impose certain requirements on the nature of the linguistic system, determining the functional basis on which it is organized; with the result that, as these early uses evolve into generalized social contexts of language use, the linguistic system is able to act through them as the means for the transmission of the culture to the child. In this way language comes to occupy the central role in the processes of social learning.

4 Language development as a semiotic process

1. Semiotic beginnings

In this chapter we shall try to summarize the child's early language learning as a sociosemiotic process. What is intended here by 'sociosemiotic' will be largely left to emerge from the discussion; but in the most general terms it is meant to imply a synthesis of three modes of interpretation, that of language in the context of the social system, that of language as an aspect of a more general semiotic, and that of the social system itself as a semiotic system— modes of interpretation that are associated with Malinowski and Firth, with Jakobson, and with Lévi-Strauss, among others. The social system, viewed in these terms, is a system of meaning relations; and these meaning relations are realized in many ways, of which one, perhaps the principal one as far as the maintenance and transmission of the system is concerned, is through their encoding in language. The meaning potential of a language, its semantic system, is therefore seen as realizing a higher level system of relations, that of the social semiotic, in just the same way as it is itself realized in the lexico-grammatical and phonological systems.

A child who is learning his mother tongue is learning how to mean. As he builds up his own meaning potential in language, he is constructing for himself a social semiotic. Since language develops as the expression of the social semiotic it serves at the same time as the means of transmitting it, and also of constantly modifying and reshaping it, as the child takes over the culture, the received system of meanings in which he is learning to share.

How early does this process begin? Many studies of language development have begun at a point when the child's 'mean length of utterance' exceeds one word; but this is already too late—the child may have a well-developed semantic system long before he begins to combine words, in fact long before he has any words at all, if by 'words' we mean lexical elements taken over from the adult language. At the other end are references to a child having a communication system at the age of a few weeks or even days; no doubt he does communicate more or less from birth, but there are significant senses in which this communication differs from language, and it is specifically language that we are concerned with here because it is language that enables him to construct a social semiotic. This does not mean that a child has no language until he has a linguistic system in the adult sense, but that there are certain features in respect of which we can say that, before a given stage, the child has not got language, and after this stage he has.

The early stages of Nigel's language development have been described to a certain degree of detail in the previous two chapters. Here we shall recapitulate the description just insofar as this is necessary to clarify the present interpretation; the relevant facts will be incorporated into the discussion.

With Nigel, the breakthrough into language occurred at the age of about nine months. At nine months old, he had a meaning system of five elements, of which two were vocalized and three realized as gestures. The two that were vocalized were

| [ø] mid-low falling to low | 'let's be together' |
| [ø] mid falling to low | 'look (it's moving)' |

The three realized gesturally were

grasping object firmly	'I want that'
touching object lightly [sic]	'I don't want that'
touching person or relevant object firmly	'do that (with it) again (e.g. make it jump up in the air)'

Here the child was on the threshold of language. Between nine and ten-and-a-half months, he developed a linguistic system. This system was set out in Fig. 1. The gestures, incidentally, disappeared by the age of twelve months.

On what grounds are we calling this a 'language'? It has no words and no structures. It is very clearly not a linguistic system in the adult sense, since it lacks the defining characteristic of such a system: it is not tri-stratal. An adult linguistic system has three strata, or levels: a semantics, a lexicogrammar (or 'syntax') and a phonology. This is what distinguishes it from all animal communication systems, which as far as we know are bi-stratal only. In similar fashion Nigel's system at this stage is bi-stratal; it has a semantics and a phonology, but nothing in between. Whether for this reason we should or should not use the terms 'semantics' and 'phonology' is not a major issue; let us say that the child has a bi-stratal proto-language consisting of meaning and sound, or a content and an expression. The elements of the system are signs in the sense of content-expression pairs.

The reasons for regarding this as a form of language are two-fold. In the first place, it has two positive features which can be used as criterial: systematicity, and functionality. There is a systematic relation between the content and the expression, and the content is interpretable in functional terms. In the second place, it shows continuity of development into the adult system. Of these it is the second point that is the more important, since it determines the relevance of the first; we know that these properties are important because they provide the essential links, the means whereby a child can grasp the nature of the adult language and interpret it as an extension of what he already has. The continuity of development, with many children (of whom Nigel was one), is not immediately apparent, if one is looking mainly at the outward manifestation of the system; but it is brought out by a consideration of the meanings, once we place these in what we are referring to as a 'sociosemiotic' context.

2. A functional semantics

In the language represented by Figure 1, the expressions are clearly not, for the most part, imitations of words or any other elements of the adult language. They are the child's own invention. In general we cannot say where they come from; ding-dong, bow-wow, yo-heave-ho and other such classical sources are probably all represented somewhere. The point is simply that they are distinct from each other; although the IPA alphabet is not, at this stage, a relevant form of notation—what is needed is a prosodic or postural notation specially designed for developmental studies— it serves to suggest what was in fact the case, that there was surprisingly little neutralization of semantic contrasts by overlap in the expression. It is likely that some children make more use of imitation in the expressions of their proto-language, using forms of words from the adult language; this is a source of difficulty for the investigator, since such forms are not at this stage being used as words (which would imply a lexicogrammatical stratum) but merely as expressions. A possible example of this is Nigel's [bø]

'I want my toy bird'; the expression may be an imitation of the *sound* of the adult pronunciation of bird but it is not the *word* bird—there are no words at this stage. It does not matter, in fact, *where* the expressions come from; their function is to signal the meanings of the child's own system.

Where then do the meanings come from? These likewise are not imitations of meanings in the adult language. They are interpretable in functional terms. The content of the system is derived from what it is the child is making the system do for him. Hence in interpreting the content we need to start with some functional-semantic hypothesis, some notion of the developmentally significant functions that, on general socio-cultural grounds (as well as from our knowledge of the nature of the adult language), we should expect to determine the content structure of the child's proto-language. For this purpose the simple framework was adopted of six basic functions; instrumental ('I want'), regulatory ('do as I tell you'), interactional ('me and you'), personal ('here I come'), heuristic ('tell me why') and imaginative ('let's pretend'). The instrumental is language as a demand for goods and services, in the satisfaction of material needs; the regulatory is language used to control the behaviour of those around, and adapt it to one's wishes. These are the more pragmatic functions. There is also a pragmatic element in the interactional, since it embodies the child's need for human contact; but there the meanings are the expression of the interaction itself, rather than of a demand for it. In its personal function, language is the expression of the child's own identity, his separateness from, and uniqueness with respect to, the environment of people and things; and this creates the context for the heuristic function, which is language in the exploration of the environment that is defined as the non-self. Finally language may function in the *creation* of an environment, an environment of the imagination that begins as pure sound and works its way up the linguistic system to become a 'let's pretend' world of songs and rhymes and stories.

Meaning is meaning *with respect to* one or other of these functions. The meanings which a small child expresses in his proto-language may be glossed by locutions in the adult language such as 'do that again' or 'nice to see you, & shall we look at this together?'; but these—like the phonetic notations referred to above—are overly specific. We cannot adequately represent what the child means by wordings such as these, or even by semantic features drawn from the adult language. What is needed is, again, some

63

sort of semantic representation that is analogously prosodic or postural. The content systems in Figure 1 are an attempt to express the meanings in systemic terms, as sets of options deriving from the functions of the initial hypothesis. The assertion is that within each of these functions the child develops a small but open-ended, indefinitely expandable, range of alternatives, and that the total set of these sets of options constitutes his semantic system at the stage in question. The functions themselves are the prototypic social contexts of the child's existence, simple semiotic structures through which he relates to and becomes a part of the social system.

If they are viewed in this light it is easy to see that there is no place for anything like an 'informative' function. The use of language in the sense of 'I've got something to tell you', which tends to obsess adults, perhaps because they have learnt it with such difficulty, is irrelevant to a small child; it has no direct social meaning. It is also inaccessible to him, since it is wholly intrinsic to language; it is a function that derives from the nature of language itself. The other six are all extralinguistic; they arise, and can be realized, independently of language, though language immeasurably extends the meaning potential that is associated with them. Nigel began with four of them simultaneously, the instrumental, regulatory, interactional and personal; after about four or five months he added the imaginative and, incipiently at least, the heuristic. Thus the functions that had been predicted were all clearly recognizable; but, unlike what might have been expected, there was no clear developmental ordering among them such that the more pragmatically oriented functions developed before the others. Non-pragmatic elements were as prominent from the start; and this became very significant when the child moved on into the next phase.

Every element showing systematic sound-meaning correspondence, and interpretable in these functional terms (these two criteria in fact defined the same set), was entered in the system, provided it was observed operationally (in a context in which it was doing a job of meaning) with a certain minimum frequency. In practice throughout the six months or so of the 'proto-language' phase, which we designate Phase I, all but two or three of the sounds provisionally interpreted as meaningful were observed with far more than minimal frequency, and, surprisingly perhaps, there was hardly any difficulty in identifying what was language and what was not. Practising was excluded, on the grounds that

64

the learning of a system is not a function of that system; Nigel did very little practising as such, but made very extensive operational use of the resources he had. (It may be that practising never is associated with the proto-language; Nigel provides no evidence either way, since he did not practise in Phase II either.) The system was reinterpreted and written up at intervals of six weeks, this being the interval which appeared to be optimal—neither so short that the account would be distorted by random non-occurrences nor so long that the system could not be seen in course of change. (See figures 1–6).

There is a marked break between NL 5 and NL 6; NL 6 may be regarded as the beginning of what we are calling 'Phase II'. Much of the remaining discussion will centre around the interpretation of what it is that is happening in Phase II; before coming on to this, however, we shall insert a brief note about the concept of situation or social context. This concept will be discussed more fully in Chapter 5.

3. Meaning and environment

A child is learning how to mean; but meaning takes place in an environment, not in solitude. What is the nature of the environment? On the one hand, it may be thought of as 'what is going on at the time': the situation in which the language is actualized and comes to life. On the other hand, it may be conceived of as the social system, with the child himself in the middle of it.

Malinowski took account of both: he called the former the 'context of situation' and the latter the 'context of culture'. Because of his interest in pragmatic speech, his characterization of the situation tended to be rather too concrete, a kind of scenario with props and stage directions; Firth replaced this with a more abstract account which allows us to interpet the situation as a generalized situation *type*, or social context. The situation is the environment of the *text*, of the meanings that are selected or 'actualized' in a given instance. The culture is the environment of the *system*, of the total meaning potential. (Hence Firth did not develop Malinowski's context of culture; his focus of attention was not on the potential but on the typical actual.) So we can start from the concept of 'situation' and define the context of culture as the set of possible situation types. This is equivalent to interpreting the social system as the total set of possible social contexts.

There is however another possible perspective, one that is complementary to this one. We can choose to define the situation by reference to the culture, instead of the other way round. We have defined the culture as a system of meanings, a semiotic system. A situation (always in the generalized sense of 'situation type') is then a semiotic structure deriving from that system.

The various 'ethnographies of speaking' that attempt to describe the relevant patterns of speech settings can be interpreted and evaluated in this light, as analyses of the semiotic structure of the situation, in its capacity as a determinant of the text. The meaning potential that a child learns to express in the first phase serves him in functions which exist independently of language, as features of human life at all times and in all cultures. But, at the same time, and in the same process, he is constructing for himself a social semiotic, a model of the culture of which he is himself a member; and he is doing so out of the semiotic properties of situations, situations in which he is a participant or an observer. The understanding of this process constitutes what Berger refers to as the 'microsociology of knowledge'—the social construction of reality from the countless microsemiotic encounters of daily life. Nigel at nine months has already embarked on this venture. His meaning potential develops as the representation of the social system and of his own place in it.

In this way a child, in the act of learning language, is also learning the culture through language. The semantic system which he is constructing becomes the primary mode of transmission of the culture. But we can also turn this point back on itself and ask the question, how has the place of language in the social system determined the nature and evolution of language? However remote this question may seem from current preoccupations— and it would not have been thought fanciful a hundred years ago— it is one that we may well bear in mind while considering how, and more especially *why*, the child makes a transition from his own proto-language into the adult linguistic system.

4. Taking over the mother tongue

Nigel continued to expand his Phase I language, extending the meaning potential within the four functions instrumental, regulatory, interactional and personal, and later adding to these a small range of meanings in the other functions. The number of distinct meanings increased as follows:

NL-1	NL-2	NL-3	NL-4	NL-5
12	21	29	32	52

Figure 5 represents the system at NL 5 (15–$16\frac{1}{2}$ months); the number of options under each heading is now

instrumental: 10   regulatory: 7   interactional: 15   personal: 16

the remaining four being 'imaginative'. Looking at the system with hindsight from the standpoint of its later development, we come to see that at least one of the options should really have been interpreted as heuristic in function. By this time, however, the functional basis of the system is itself beginning to evolve into a new phase.

By NL 5, therefore, the system has expanded to something like four or five times its original measure of potential. Essentially, though, it is still a system of the same kind. The meanings continue to form a simple semantic taxonomy—with one small but extremely significant exception, which foreshadows things to come:

$$
\left\{
\begin{array}{l}
\longrightarrow \left[\begin{array}{ll}
\text{Anna} & \text{an:a} \\
\text{Mummy} & \text{ama} \\
\text{Daddy} & \text{dada}
\end{array}\right. \\
\longrightarrow \left[\begin{array}{lll}
\text{seeking} & \text{——} & \text{(mid-high + high, level)} \\
\text{finding} & \text{\\——} & \text{(mid fall + low level)}
\end{array}\right.
\end{array}
\right.
$$

Here we have for the first time the intersection of two semantic systems, two simultaneous sets of options in free combination. Apart from this, Nigel can still only mean one thing at once.

Then, with quite dramatic suddenness, Nigel abandoned the glossogenic process. He stopped creating language for himself, and began to use the one he heard around him. This is the transitional stage we are referring to as Phase II. It corresponds to what is more usually regarded as the beginnings of language, because it is the point at which vocabulary (in the true sense, as distinct from imitations of word sounds) and structure start to appear; but from the present standpoint it is already transitional.

The changes that characterize Phase II were summarized in Chapter 3. Nigel learnt grammar, and he learnt dialogue. That is to say: 1) he replaced his own bi-stratal (content, expression) system by the adult tri-stratal system (content, form, expression, i.e., semantics, lexicogrammar, phonology); 2) he replaced his own one-way (monologue) system by the adult two-way system (dialogue). These processes began in NL 6 and were well established in NL 7 (18–19½ months). They are the two critical steps into the adult linguistic system; we will explain and illustrate them in turn.

5. Lexicogrammatical and semantic structures

Lexicogrammar is, in folk-linguistic terminology, the level of 'wording' in language that comes between meaning and sounding; it is grammar and vocabulary. Meanings are no longer output directly as sounds; they are first coded in lexicogrammatical forms and then recoded in sounds. The outward sign of a grammar is structures; that of a vocabulary is words, or lexical items. There is no very clear line between the meanings that are coded as grammatical structures and those that are coded as lexical items; the latter represent, as a rule, the more specific or more 'delicate' options. By the end of NL 7 Nigel had a vocabulary probably amounting to some two hundred words, together with the structures represented in the following examples:

gɹì . . . gɹī: là	green . . . green light
dâ . . . dā: dɔ̀bɪ	tiny . . . tiny toothpick
ɔ̄lō͏ʷ tí:ko:	hello teacosy
gɹī: kà	green car

All these appeared on the same day, which was the first day on which he had used any structures at all (on the criterion of intonation, i.e. composite forms on a single tone contour). These were followed next day by

gɹ:ī: kà . . . bl:ū̄: kà . . . ān̯̂ʰ	green car . . . blue car . . . another
mɔ̄: mì ˀ	more meat
mɔ̄: mì ˀ plɪ	more meat please
t͡ʉ̄: bɔ̀kʷ	two books

and within a week by green peg, more omelette, and two plus various items including lorries, trains and helicopters. In addition there were the following narratives, which form structures at the semantic level but not yet at the lexicogrammatical level:

ⁿdà̄ⁿda . . . pà̀ɪ . . . [blowing]ɸʷ . . . t̯ôy̯a	uncle . . . pipe . . . smoke . . . (like) train
ˀɔ̂ˀ . . . tɹì . . . tɛkəwè: . . . ōgɔ̀ . . . babā	broken . . . tree . . . take-away . . . all-gone . . . bye-bye
bɹ̩̄kè̀ . . . ōdɪɔ̀ . . . m̩̄q̯ . . . dàda	breakfast . . . oh-dear (I'm hungry) . . . milk . . . (and some for) Daddy
t͡ʃɔ̀y̯ā . . . là . . . gɹì	train . . . light . . . green

68

At this stage, the lexical items combine freely in semantic structures. They combine only with partial freedom into grammatical structures; <u>more</u>, for example, combines freely with items of food, including countables such as <u>more cherries</u>, but it does not yet combine with cars or trains. The explanation of this will appear below.

6. Interactional patterns

Dialogue is the taking on oneself, and assigning to others, of social roles of a special kind, namely those that are defined by language—the speech roles of ordering, questioning, responding and the like. Nigel had launched into dialogue just four weeks before his first structures appeared; here are some more early examples (cf Chapter 3, section 6):

NIGEL: ádᵛdà 'What's that?' MOTHER: That's a plug. NIGEL [imitating]: lı̀koba . . . ádᵛdà MOTHER: That's a chain. NIGEL: ʦ̀ʉ́ʦ̀ʉ̀ MOTHER: No—not a train, a chain. NIGEL [pointing to line drawn on side of bottle]: ádᵛdà MOTHER: That's a line. NIGEL: ɹaːɹa: [roaring, i.e. 'a lion']

MOTHER: Take the toothpaste to Daddy and go and get your bib. NIGEL [doing so] dàda . . . n̄ıǹn̄ıǹ . . . ʦ̀ʉ́ʦ̀ʉ̀ 'Daddy . . . (give) noddy (toothpaste to him) . . . (get the bib with the) train (picture on it)'

ANNA: We're going out for a walk, and we'll go and get some fish. NIGEL [hopefully] tı̀kɔ '(And we'll get some) sticks' ANNA: No, we're not getting any sticks today. NIGEL [plaintively]: lɔ́ᵘ '(Aren't we going to look for) holes?', or '(What can I put in the) holes?'

NIGEL [coming into study]: ɜ̄ ē ɛ̄ ɜ̄ ɜ̄ bɔ̀uwɔ̀u 'I want to (come and) draw (originally = 'draw dogs') (with you)' FATHER: No, I'm working. NIGEL: dādıkədà '(You're) playing the tabla' FATHER: No I'm not playing dadıkada; I'm writing. NIGEL: bɔ̀uwɔ̀u '(You're) drawing'

MOTHER [pointing]: Who's that? NIGEL: nːā 'Anna' MOTHER [pointing to self]: And who's that? NIGEL: mā 'Mummy' MOTHER [pointing to Nigel]: And who's that? NIGEL: nı̄ 'Nigel'

FATHER: Where's my pudding? [Five minutes later it is brought in] NIGEL: dɛ̀ə 'There'

If we analyze these specimens of dialogue in terms of Nigel's speech role potential, we find that he can:

(1) respond to a WH-question (provided he knows that the answer is already known to the questioner);

(2) respond to a command, acting it out and verbalizing as he does so;

(3) respond to a statement, signalling attention and continuing the conversation;

(4) respond to a response to something he himself has said; and

(5) ask a WH-question (but only one, namely 'What's that?').

This last is the only option he has for demanding a specifically linguistic response, and thus for *initiating* dialogue. It is important to stress that dialogue is interpreted as the exchange of *speech* roles; that is, it is language in functions that are created and defined by language itself, such as asking and answering questions. A response such as 'Yes do' to 'Shall I . . . ?', or 'Yes I do' to 'Do you want . . . ?', is not an instance of dialogue, since the responses are still extralinguistic in function; they express simple instrumental or regulatory meanings. Early in Phase I Nigel could already mean 'yes' and 'no' in such contexts, where they were fully interpretable in terms of his elementary functions; but he *could not answer a yes/no question*—because he could not use language to give information, to communicate experience to someone who had not shared that experience with him. It is for exactly the same reason that he cannot answer a WH-question unless he sees that the answer is available to the questioner also.

Communicating new information, as we have stressed, is a complex notion, since it is a function of language that is wholly brought about and defined by language itself. Hence it is conceptualizable only at a very late stage. Nigel did not grasp it until towards the end of Phase II, when he was completing the transition to the adult language system. When he did grasp it, he superimposed a further semantic distinction of his own, between imparting information that was new and verbalizing information that was already known and shared. Since at this time he controlled the grammatical system of declarative/interrogative, but not yet the semantic system of statement/(yes/no) question, he adapted the grammatical distinction to his own use: the verbalizing of shared information was realized by the declarative and the communicating of new information by the interrogative. So, for example, on being given a present by his uncle, he turned to his mother who was present and said <u>Uncle gave you some marbles</u> (i.e. 'you saw that Uncle gave me some marbles'; <u>you</u> = 'me' regularly throughout this stage). He then ran out to show his father, who had not been present, and said <u>Daddy, did Uncle give you some marbles?</u> (i.e. 'you didn't see, but Uncle gave me some marbles').

If utterances such as those we have illustrated are not communicating information, what are they doing? In the context of *culture*, of course, they are communicating information. As Mary Douglas puts it, 'If we ask of any form of communication the simple question what is being communicated? The answer is: information from the social system. The exchanges which are being communicated constitute the social system'. This is exactly the social semiotic perspective which we are adopting here. But in the context of *situation* their function is not the communication of information to a hearer for whom it is new. Some of the utterances the child produces are clearly pragmatic in function: <u>more meat</u> means 'I want some more meat'. But others cannot be accounted for in this way, and we must look for some other interpretation. First, however, let us attempt a reconsideration of the significance of the second phase in Nigel's language development. Why does the child abandon his own language-creating efforts in favour of the mother tongue? And, in particular, why does he take the specific steps of building in a grammar and learning dialogue?

7. Limitations of Phase I system

The essential motivation behind both these moves can be seen in the inherent functional limitations of the child's Phase I system. It can no longer meet the requirements of his own social semiotic. Does this mean that it cannot express enough differentiation in meaning? In the long run, this is certainly true; but when Nigel moved into Phase II he was still very far from having exhausted the potential of his Phase I system—he could have added many more elements without undue strain on his own articulatory or his hearer's auditory resources. There is however a much more fundamental limitation on the proto-language, which is that *it is impossible to mean more than one thing at once*. This can be done only by the interpolation of a lexicogrammatical stratum. The reason for this is that, in order for different meanings to be mapped on to one another and output in the form of single, integrated structures, there has to be an intermediate level of coding in between the meanings and the sounds. This function is served by the lexicogrammar.

So for example when Nigel says [lɔ̌ᵘ], the meaning is already complex: something like 'there are holes—and something must be done about them'. His experience as an observer of holes is expressed in the articulation [lɔᵘ], and his personal stake in the matter, his own intrusion into the situation, is expressed by the rising tone and plaintive voice quality. This is possible only because he now has a coding level of grammar and lexis, a relational system lying not at the semantic or phonological interfaces but at the heart of language, a level of purely linguistic abstractions serving as an intermediary in what Lamb used to call the 'transduction' of meanings into sounds. This system can accept meanings derived from different functional origins and encode them into unified lexicogrammatical constructs, which are then output as 'wordings'—patterns of ordering, word selections, intonation patterns and the like.

The example we have just given shows this functional semantic mapping in its simplest form. The expression [lɔ̌ᵘ] represents a combination of the two most general functional components of meaning, the *ideational* (Bühler's 'representational', Lyons' 'cognitive', Hymes' 'referential') and the *interpersonal* (Bühler's 'conative' and 'expressive', Lyons' 'social', Hymes' 'socioexpressive' or 'stylistic'). The former is the observer function of language; it is the speaker reflecting on his environment. The latter is the intruder function of language; it is the speaker acting on his environment. It is a property of the adult language that it enables the speaker to do both these things at once—in fact it makes it impossible for him not to, though in infinitely varied and indirect ways towards which Nigel's utterance is no more than the first crude striving. But essentially this is what he is striving after: a plurifunctional system that enables him to mean more than one thing at once. It is for this that he needs a grammar.

By the same token, he needs a grammar in order to be able to engage in dialogue. Dialogue involves just this kind of functional mapping, of content elements on to situational elements; the same structure expresses both an ideational meaning, in terms of the speaker's experience, and an interpersonal meaning in terms of the speaker's adoption and assignment of speech roles. In the adult linguistic system, this requirement is embodied in the systems of transitivity and of mood. Transitivity expresses the speaker's experience of process in the external world, and mood expresses his structuring of the speech situation; as sets of options, the two are quite independent, but they combine to form integrated lexicogrammatical structures. Nigel is still far from having either a transitivity system or a mood system. But he is beginning to interact linguistically, and to build up a potential for dialogue.

Thus it is not the fact that his Phase I 'proto-language' cannot be understood by other people that provides the impetus for the move into Phase II. There is no sign yet that he wants to interact verbally with people other than those in his immediate environment, who understand him perfectly well; but he does want to *interact* with them, and his proto-language does not allow for this. A simple exchange of verbal signals can, of course, be prolonged indefinitely in the proto-language, and often is; but it is impossible to engage in dynamic role play. The system cannot provide for the adoption, assignment, acceptance and rejection of speech roles.

Here is one brief example showing the sort of multiple meaning and multiple role-playing that Nigel has mastered by the time he is well on into Phase II; it is taken from NL 9 (21–22½ months):

NIGEL [having fallen and hurt himself earlier in the day; feeling his forehead]: ádᵛdà 'What's that?' FATHER: That's plaster, sticking plaster. NIGEL: tell Mummy take it òff '(I'm going to) . . .' . . . [running to Mother] take it óff 'take it off!'

8. Pragmatic and mathetic

We can now interpret the strategy that Nigel adopted as the basis of Phase II. In Section 4 above we cited the first instance of the breakdown of the simple semantic taxonomy that characterizes the Phase I language: the combination of naming a person (one person or another) and interacting with that person (in one way or another), e.g. [ān:a] 'Anna, where are you?'. This is exactly the same phenomenon as was illustrated in the last section, where the meaning of [lɔ́ᵘ] was 'there are holes—and something must be done about them'; another early example was [kᵛē:kᵛ], said on seeing a cake in the middle of the table and meaning 'that's cake—and I want some!'.

All these provide a preview of what is to come. If we look at the meanings of Nigel's Phase II utterances in functional terms, we find him apparently generalizing, out of the initial set of developmental functions which were recognizable in Phase I, two broad functional categories, or 'macro-functions' as we might call them: one of them demanding a response, the other not. The response that is demanded is, at first, in terms of goods and services: 'I want that', 'do that again' and so on; increasingly however it becomes a demand for a verbal response, e.g. 'what's that?'. The other type of utterance, which demands no response, involves at first the observation, recall or prediction of phenomena seen or heard: 'I can see/hear', 'I saw/heard', 'I shall see/hear'; it then extends to narrative and descriptive contexts.

The first category clearly derives from the instrumental and regulatory systems of Phase I, and also in part the interactional; functionally we are calling it *pragmatic*. The developmental history of the second category was much more difficult to follow; but it can be shown to derive, by an interesting and indirect route, from the interactional, in its non-pragmatic aspect, the personal, and the heuristic functions—the last of which we can see emerging in the later stages of Phase I when we look back at these from a Phase II vantage point. This appears to happen somewhat as follows (cf. p. 44). Nigel begins (NL 1–2) by using some external object, typically a picture, as a channel for interaction with others; hence the gloss 'nice to see you—& shall we look at this together?'. He then (NL 3) separates the interactional from the personal element, the former developing into forms of greeting and the latter into 'self' expressions of interest, pleasure and the like. Then, as the split between the self and the environment becomes clearer, the inter-actional element reappears on a higher level, the attention being focussed on an external object which the other person is required to name (NL 4–5): 'look at this—now you say its name'. At first this is used only when the object is familiar—again, typically a picture—and the name already (receptively) known; it then splits into two meanings one of which is a demand for a new name, one that is not known, the 'what's that?' form illustrated earlier. The words that name objects are at the same time being learnt produc-tively, and are then used in the encoding of expressions of personal interest and involvement: 'look, that's a . . .!'. Thus out of a combination of the personal (self-oriented) and the heuristic (environment-oriented) functions of Phase I there arises a general-ized nonpragmatic mode of meaning which is in contrast to the pragmatic mode identified above.

What is the function of such 'non-pragmatic' utterances? Can we characterize their meaning in positive terms? Lewis already observed this distinction some forty years ago; he uses the term 'manipulative' for the pragmatic function, and labels the other 'declarative'. This is adequate as a description, but does not really explain what these utterances mean. Lewis appears to interpret 'declarative' in terms of self-expression, and the demand for an expressive response. It seems, however, that the function of utterances which are not pragmatic is essentially a learning one. It arises, like the pragmatic function, by a process of generalization from the initial set of extrinsic functions of Phase I; and it is complementary to it, as reflection is to action. We have suggested referring to it as the *mathetic* function; it is language enabling the child to learn about his social and material environment, serving him in the construction of reality. This function is realized, in the first instance, through the child's observing, recalling and predicting the objects and events which impinge on his perceptions.

At the beginning of Phase II, all utterances are *either* one thing *or* the other: either pragmatic or mathetic. And when we look at the new lexical items coming in to Nigel's system in NL 6–7, we find that the majority, probably more than three-quarters of them, come in in the context of the mathetic function, not the pragmatic. (Moreover, each word, and each structure, is at first specialized to one function only; they are not used in both.) This is partly explainable by reference to the greater situational dependence of the pragmatic mode; where the meaning is 'I want . . .', the speaker can often point to what it is he wants, so that Nigel continued to use the unmarked instrumental and regulatory options of Phase I well on into Phase II. But the observation also recalls Lévi-Strauss's remark that in all cultures 'the universe is an object of thought at least as much as it is a means of satisfying needs'. We find this to be already a determining factor in the child's language development; language evolves in the context of his thinking about the universe no less than in the context of his exploiting it.

9. Phase II functional strategy

It is largely thanks to Nigel himself that this aspect of his Phase II strategy, the contrast between a mathetic and a pragmatic mode, can be asserted with relative confidence. At a particular moment— the last week of NL 7, one week after the structural explosion discussed in Section 5—he adopted the intonational distinction of rising/falling, which he then kept up for some months. It was noticeable that, from that date on, every utterance had one tone contour, and that the tone was either clearly rising or clearly falling in every instance. The interpretation soon became apparent. All falling tone utterances were mathetic in function, and all rising tone utterances were pragmatic in function. Some examples from NL 7–8:

PRAGMATIC

chuffa stúck 'the train's stuck; help me to get it out'
high wáll 'let me jump off and you catch me'
háve it 'I want that'
play ráo 'let's play at lions'
squeeze órange 'squeeze the orange'
bounce táble 'I want to bounce the orange on the table, can I?'
water ón 'I want the water turned on'
Anna help gréenpea 'Anna help me to eat the greenpeas'
Dada come overthere nów 'Daddy come over there now'
make cross tíckmatick . . . in Dada róom 'I want to make a
  cross on the typewriter in Daddy's room'
chuffa under túnnel . . . getit fóryou 'the train's in the tunnel;
  get it for me'
play rao bártok 'I want to play at lions with me holding the
  sleeve of the Bartok record'

MATHETIC

molasses nòse 'I've got molasses on my nose'
red swèater 'that's a red sweater'
chuffa stòp 'the train's stopped'
loud Dvòřak 'that a loud bit of the Dvořak record'
green stick fìnd 'the green stick's been found'
Dada black brùsh 'that's Daddy's black brush'
man clean càr 'the man was cleaning his car'
Anna make noise gràss 'Anna made a noise with a piece of
  grass'
clever boy fix roof on lòrry 'this clever boy fixed the roof on
  the lorry'
Dada come bàck . . . Dada come on fast chùffa 'Daddy's come
  back; Daddy came on a fast train'
too dàrk . . . open cùrtain . . . lìght now 'it was too dark;
  you've opened the curtains, and it's light now'

It may be pointed out that some of these utterances could be
translated into either pragmatic or mathetic forms. But Nigel
himself made the distinction clear. If the tone was rising, he was
not satisfied until some response was forthcoming; whereas if the
tone was falling, no response was expected. The following is a
typical example showing both types of utterance, the one followed
by the other:

Dada got scrambled ègg . . . Mummy get fóryou scrambled egg
'Daddy's got some scrambled egg; Mummy get some
scrambled egg for me!'

Thus Nigel developed a clear functional strategy for Phase II, the
phase that is transitional between his own proto-language and the
language of the adult system. In what sense is it transitional? Here
we come back once more to the sociosemiotic perspective. Phase II
is defined as the period of mastering the adult language *system*;
the end of Phase II is defined as the point when he has effectively
mastered the system and can continue unhindered in his mastery
of the language. It is unlikely that this point can be tied to any
particular moment in time, but in Nigel's case it coincides
roughly with the end of his second year, around NL 10 in the
present study. The notion of transition, however, is perhaps more
readily interpretable in functional terms. At the beginning of
Phase II, it is 'each utterance one function'. This is what makes
it possible for Nigel to put the intonation contrast to systematic use
in the way he does (he cannot of course use it in the way English
does, because the systems that are realized by intonation in
English are as yet beyond his functional potential). Gradually in
the course of Phase II he moves on, through a stage of 'each
utterance typically one principal function, the other subsidiary',
to a final stage of 'every utterance all functions'. This is the
pattern that is characteristic of the adult language.

How does this functional development take place? Not in the
obvious way, which would be by some sort of transcategorization
process in which sentence types were transferred out of one box
into another. It happens through a reinterpretation of the concept
of function on to a more abstract level, such that it becomes the
organizing principle of the linguistic system itself. We could express
this by saying that the 'functions' of Phase I become 'macro-
functions' in Phase II and 'meta-functions' in Phase III.

This, it seems, is the developmental source of the functional components of the adult linguistic system, the ideational and interpersonal referred to above. Whatever the specific *use* to which
language is being put—and by the end of Phase II the child has
indefinitely many uses of language (because they are indefinitely
subclassifiable)—in all contexts the speaker has to be both obseiver
and intruder at the same time. It is the pragmatic function that
has provided the main context for the 'intruder' systems of mood,
modality, intensity, person and the like, and the mathetic function

that has provided the main context for the 'observer' systems of transitivity, extent and location, quantifying and qualifying, and so on. But it is characteristic of the adult that, whatever the social context, the expression of his meanings in language involves both reflection on and interaction with the social system.

Hence in the course of Phase II the notion of 'function' becomes totally distinct from that of 'use'. The adult has unlimited uses for language; but the typical adult utterance, whatever its use, has an ideational and an interpersonal component of meaning. At the same time, these 'metafunctional' components of the adult language arise, however indirectly, out of the primary developmental functions of Phase I, where function was synonymous with use. It is in Phase II that the child makes the fundamental discovery that he can mean two things at once—he can both observe and interact with his environment at the same time; when he enters Phase III, all uses of language are mediated through this twofold meaning potential. The elementary functional contexts in which he first constructed his own proto-language are still there; they have evolved into the semiotic structures that we recognize as situations and settings of language use. What has changed is the meaning potential that he can deploy as an actor.

A schematic representation of the process of systemic-functional development as we have postulated it is given in Figure 7.

10. Continuity of the developmental process

It is not easy to say how much of Nigel's language learning strategies represents a general pattern of transition into the adult language system, and how much is merely his own way through. Clearly the use of intonation to realize the pragmatic/mathetic distinction is an individual device; but the distinction itself may be a general feature—at least there seems nothing to suggest that it could not be. It is quite possible, on the other hand, that many children do not bother to create a Phase I language at all; almost certainly they do not all display Nigel's dramatic shift from Phase I to Phase II. But one has to be careful here. It is clear that there is no single origin for the expressions of the proto-language, and it could well be that some children already use imitations of adult sounds in this context; these would then appear to be words, although they would not in fact be functioning as items of vocabulary—there would still be no lexicogrammatical level in the system. Moreover many children use the holophrase as a transitional strategy, which makes the introduction of the lexico-grammar a much less sudden affair.

However that may be, the point to be emphasized here is that of continuity, not discontinuity. There is, with Nigel, a discontinuity in the expression, as well as, of course, the discontinuity that arises from the introduction of a third level of coding into the system. But there is no discontinuity in the content. The social functions that have determined the proto-language—satisfying immediate needs, controlling people's behaviour, being 'together', expressing the uniqueness of the self, exploring the world of the non-self and creating a world in the imagination—all these evolve gradually and naturally into the social contexts and situation types that we characterize as semiotic structures; and the semantic systems, the meaning potential that derives from these functions, evolve likewise. The progressive approximation of the child's meanings to those of the adult, through interaction with and reinforcement by older speakers, begins before these meanings are (necessarily) realized through the words and structures of the adult language, and continues without interruption. Without this continuity, the semantic system could not function effectively in the transmission of the social system from the adult to the child.

It is the essential continuity of the process of 'learning how to mean', however early this process is considered to start, that we hope to bring out by adopting a sociosemiotic perspective. Our object of study here is still language; but it seems that additional light can be shed on language, especially where language development is concerned, if it is placed in the wider context of the social system considered as a system of meanings—hence the concept of language as 'social semiotic'. From another point of view, this is a means of bringing together the sociolinguistic and the semantic interpretations of language development, which at present remain rather unconnected. From the sociolinguistic standpoint, learning the mother tongue has been interpreted as the progressive mastery of a 'communicative competence', the use of language in different social contexts. But the notion of communicative competence, though valuable as a temporary structure, a heuristic device for comparative developmental and educational studies, does not relate to the nature of the linguistic system, or explain how and why the child learns it. Work in developmental semantics has focussed mainly on the child's learning of the word meanings and other specific aspects of the ideational component of the adult linguistic system. But these studies do not in general relate the system to its social contexts or to the functions that language serves in the young child's life. Each of these fields of investigation constitutes, needless to say, an essential element in the total picture. But they need to be brought together, through some framework that does not separate the system from its use, or meaning from social context.

We have been perhaps too readily persuaded to accept dichotomies of this kind, with their implication that an interactional or 'socio-' perspective is one in which the focus is on behaviour, performance, the use of the system 'as opposed to' the system itself. It is useful to be reminded that there are also sociological explanations, and that an interpretation of language as interaction is complementary to, and no less explanatory than, a view of language as knowledge.

A child learns a symbolic behaviour potential; this is what he 'can mean', in terms of a few elementary social functions. In the process he creates a language, a system of meanings deriving from these functions, together with their realizations in sound. The meanings are, in turn, the encoding of the higher-level meanings that constitute the developing child's social system; first his own relationships with people and objects, then the relationships among the people and objects themselves, then relationships among the symbols, and so on. In the process there comes a moment when the child abandons the glossogenic trail—which we may speculate on as a model of the evolutionary path of human language—and settles for the 'mother tongue', the language he hears from others. With this, given its potential for dialogue and for multiple meaning, he can engage in an ongoing polyphonic interaction with those around him.

Since the fact that language encodes the social system has in the long run determined the form of its internal organization, the child faces no sharp discontinuity at this point; he is taking over a system that is a natural extension of that which he has constructed for himself. His own functional semiotic now reappears at a more abstract level at the core of the adult language, in the ideational and interpersonal components of the semantic system. All linguistic interaction comes to be mediated through these two functions; and since they are not just aspects of the use of language, but are at the basis of the system itself, every actual instance of linguistic interaction has meaning not only in particular but also in general, as an expression of the social system and of the child's place in it—in other words, it is related to the context of culture as well as to the

80

context of the situation. This explains how in the course of learning language a child is also all the time learning *through* language; how the microsemiotic exchanges of family and peer group life contain within themselves indices of the most pervasive semiotic patterns of the culture.

5 Into the adult language

1. Reality at nine months (NL 1)

Here we shall try to take further the interpretation of Nigel's progress through Phase II, the transition from his own proto-language into the mother tongue. In Phase I, Nigel had constructed a semiotic based on the primary distinction between himself and the rest of reality, the environment of people and of things.

This pattern begins to emerge already at NL 1, and underlies the functional system that was discussed at the beginning. At that stage, Nigel's semiotic universe consists of a self and a non-self, the environment; the environment consists of persons and of objects; and the persons figure in the two contexts of interaction and of control.

I. THE SELF. The meanings that are associated with the self ('personal' function) realize the states and processes of his own consciousness. The orientation may be either inward (withdrawal into the self: 'I'm sleepy') or outward; within the latter there is a distinction between the affect function (pleasure, in general and specifically focussed on taste) and the curiosity function (interest, in general and specifically focussed on movement).

II. THE ENVIRONMENT: (a) persons: (i) interaction. The persons in the environment figure in two semiotic roles. In a context of interaction ('interactional' function), the meaning is one of rapport, with the mother or other key person. The first move may be made by the child himself (initiation) or by the other party (response); in either case there is an exchange of meanings between them.

II. THE ENVIRONMENT: (a) persons: (ii) control. In a context of control ('regulatory' function), the meanings express the role of the

82

other as acceding to the will of the self; this is the child's incipient mode of social control.

II. THE ENVIRONMENT: (*b*) *objects*. The meanings associated with objects ('instrumental' function) realize a demand for possession. There is just one generalized demand, 'I want that'; with the exception that one favourite object is singled out for specific request. This object—in Nigel's case a toy bird, always kept in one spot—stands for the constancy of the environment; it is a symbol of permanence, and it has a request form unique to itself, 'I want my bird'.

At this stage Nigel's semiotic interaction with other persons is channelled through some object; typically an object that is itself symbolic, a picture. There is a kind of natural dialectic here, since it is also true that this effective interaction with objects takes place through symbolic interaction with persons: they give him things, make them jump for him, and so on. Hence the 'other' in the environment enters into all the non-self contexts, but in different guises: as be-er (interactional), as doer (regulatory), and as giver (instrumental). The child himself takes on the complementary roles of, respectively, be-er, causer, and recipient; and this anticipates in an interesting way the roles of persons in the transitivity system of the adult semantic.

Nigel's model of reality at NL 1 (9–10½ months), as we apprehend it from a study of his semantic system, is somewhere along these lines (the semantic functions are shown in parenthesis):

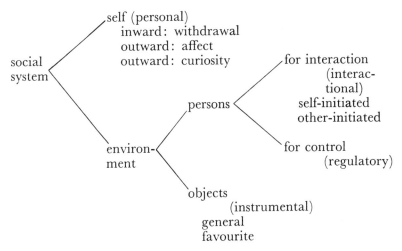

2. Nine to fifteen months (NL 1–5)

This is a socially constructed model of reality. It has been built up in the course of interaction with others, through semiotic exchanges between Nigel and those around him.

Over the next six months, up to NL 5 (15–16½ months), the picture is broadened and refined at all points. New meanings are added and details are filled in. But it remains essentially a model of the same *kind*. The main headings are still the same, though the content of each has significantly expanded.

NL 5 represents the highest point of the Phase I system, when Nigel is about to launch into the transition to the adult language. By NL 5 the picture is as follows:

I. THE SELF. The semiotic projection of the self still takes the forms of reaction to and curiosity about the environment. By NL 4 the affective category, at first restricted to an expression of delight, has specified out into a small number of distinct meanings, of pleasure, excitement, disgust, and impatience. In the same period the curiosity function has extended beyond simple movement to particular classes of objects that are auditorily and visually prominent—aeroplane, dog, ball, bird and bus. The general meaning of curiosity, the outward focussing of the self in the form of attention to a particular object, remains at the forefront of the semantic system throughout this period; it is also closely tied up with interactional meanings in which the self's relationship with another person is realized through *shared* attention to an object—typically, with Nigel at all times, a picture, which is inherently a symbolic object.

II. THE ENVIRONMENT: (*a*) *persons:* (*i*) *interaction.* Very early on (NL 2, 10½–12 months), Nigel starts to mean individuals—the three that form part of his social system, Anna, Daddy, Mummy (appearing in that order); and he distinguishes these from all other meanings by the use of a clearly marked high level tone—all other meanings are expressed on some kind of falling tone. He can both initiate and respond to greetings, and he develops specific responses in other contexts—to calls, and to reproofs. But the major development here is that of the orientation of interaction, where two distinct emphases emerge. Probably the most frequent of all Nigel's vocalizations in early Phase I is that glossed as 'nice to see you; & shall we look at this together?', interaction with an individual that is channelled through shared attention to an object. From NL 2 onwards, this may focus in either of two ways. It may focus more on the person, with the interaction itself in the forefront; or it may focus more on the object, and this becomes, more and more clearly as time goes on, a demand for a *name*, with a meaning something like 'look at this (picture); now you say the name' (it being understood that the picture is a familiar one and the name of the object already known). The latter meaning is less purely interactional, and is closely linked to the personal meaning of general interest or curiosity, with the sense of 'look: that's interesting'—where, however, the object of attention is not necessarily a picture, and no response is demanded. In this area Nigel also displays his first awareness of 'texture', of meanings in the environment of other meanings: he comes to distinguish the first occurrence 'what's that?' (mid level + mid fall, no upjump) from subsequent occurrences '& what's *that*?' (mid level + high fall, with upjump).

II. THE ENVIRONMENT: (*a*) *persons:* (*ii*) *control.* Nigel's basic system of general regulatory meanings remains in force throughout Phase I, expanding to include responses to offers, both positive and negative ('Shall I . . .?'—'Yes'/'No'), and also one or two specific meanings embodying a request for action, or, more often, for joint action, such as 'pull the curtains', 'let's draw a picture', 'let's go for a walk'. The most frequent control forms, however, are still the general ones whose meaning depends on the situation: 'do that', 'do that again'.

II. THE ENVIRONMENT: (*b*) *objects.* Requests for objects continue to be mainly dependent on the context; but the specific demand for a favourite object remains and expands into a demand for objects of a ritual kind, having symbolic value with reference to himself or some other person ('pottie', 'powder', 'clock'). Nigel adds a response to offers ('Do you want (me to) . . .?'—'Yes'), distinguishing as always, though with decreasing consistency, between regulatory meanings, demanding behaviour on the part of a specific individual, and instrumental ones, demanding a particular object or service; and in the latter connection he adds another distinction, that between asking for a thing that is visible (goods that are there) and asking for a thing that is not visible (services, and goods that are not there).

3. The picture at the end of Phase I (NL 5)

So when we come to NL 5, at the very end of Phase I, when Nigel is about to launch into the adult system, we find that the pragmatic modes, the instrumental and regulatory, have reached a stage where they embody a number of different kinds of demand: typically, instrumental 'give me', 'show me', 'help me', regulatory 'do this', 'let's do this', and perhaps the first signs of a third, 'let me do this', i.e. 'I want to be allowed to . . .', 'can I . . .?'. The number of different specific demands within each type is however quite small, since in most cases of pragmatic speech the context will serve: 'give me that (thing there)', 'show me that (thing you're holding)', 'do that (which you were going) again', and so on. The specific objects that come to be demanded 'by name' are (i) items of food, and (ii) ritual objects.

By contrast, the interactional and personal modes are considerably expanded. In the former, we find (i) generalized greeting 'hullo!' and response 'and hullo to you!'; (ii) shared attention, as before, now contrasting with shared regret 'look it's broken—let's be sad together'; (iii) three responses to verbal interaction, to 'where's . . .?', to 'say . . .', and to 'look at . . .'; and (iv) personalized greetings which are now systemically complex, since two meaning systems intersect: 'Mummy/Daddy/Anna' and 'seeking (where are you?)/finding (there you are!)'. This, as noted earlier, is the first breakaway from the simple semantic taxonomy, and indicates the origin of grammar, the introduction of a level of coding intermediate between context and expression.

In the personal function, the number of thing-names has now increased to eight, five characterized by prominence (movement or noise) and three as simply familiar objects (ball, stick, teddy). This is the origin of vocabulary; and it marks the beginning of the stage of observation, recall and prediction which we can interpret as heuristic in function—or, in the terms we have adopted for Phase II, as 'mathetic'. At the same time, however, there is a sudden final burst of energy in the Phase I system, with no less than eight distinct 'baby words' expressing different kinds of interest and emotion. It is intriguing that this happens just when Nigel is about to begin the transition into the adult semiotic mode, as if it was Nigel's ceremonial farewell to semiotic infancy.

Finally at NL 5 we find a small number of other elements, of the type of games, pretends and jingles, that represent meaning as a form of play. This is the imaginative function in its inception, and it remains a subsidiary but lively motif through Phase II and into the adult language. The early semiotics of play, verbal and non-verbal, is a rather neglected aspect of language development studies, and one that we have not attempted to cover here; but it is a field which needs to be investigated already at the pre-mother tongue stage.

4. Continuity into Phase II (NL 6)

We have emphasized throughout the twin themes of discontinuity and continuity: discontinuity in the linguistic system, with the major evolutionary change that takes place when the child shifts into the three-level system of the adult language, combined with continuity at the phonetic and semantic ends of the system. With the quite startlingly sudden leap that Nigel took into Phase II, it is all the more striking to find an essential semantic continuity linking the new modes of meaning with those of Phase I. Yet the continuity is clearly there. Nigel does not throw away the meaning potential he has built up for himself in Phase I, nor does he abandon and begin again the definition of the social contexts of language use. He continues along essentially the same path as before, so that the mother tongue comes in as a natural extension of the baby language.

What Nigel does, as we have seen, is to generalize out of the Phase I functional contexts a distinction between two semiotic modes, the pragmatic and the mathetic—language as action, and language as reflection. At first, different words and structures tend to be associated with each, reflecting the two different kinds of meaning that are involved. There is also a third, subsidiary theme of language as creation, or meaning in the imaginative mode.

Nigel expressed the systematic distinction between the two major modes by means of the phonological opposition between falling and rising tone: pragmatic ('response required') as rising tone, mathetic ('response not required') as falling tone. The falling tone was a direct continuation of the dominant intonation pattern of Phase I, where all tones were falling except in one interactional system, that of individualized greetings (personal names), which was first high level and then systematically either mid level stepping up to high level ('where are you?') or high fall followed by low level ('there you are!'). The rising tone evolved in a very striking way in the middle of NL 7, at 19 months, by a progression from falling, through narrow falling, then level, to rising: \ —⌐ —/, the whole process taking place within one week. From then on the two tones were in systemic contrast and remained so for the rest of Phase II and into Phase III. In a number of instances Nigel said what was in other respects 'the same thing' on both tones, one after the other, with consequent differences in meaning; we have cited the example of tell mummy take it òff . . . take it óff ('I'm going to tell Mummy to take it off . . . [running to Mother] take it off!'). The semantics of the system is made explicit by Nigel's imposing on the communication process a formal signal that he does, or else does not, require a response. In time the response that is required comes to be more and more often a verbal one.

At first each utterance is *either* pragmatic *or* mathetic; but gradually, by a reinterpretation of the nature of 'function' such that it becomes not just a generalized context of use but the central organizing principle of the entire semantic system, by the end of Phase II a point is reached where every utterance is *both* pragmatic *and* mathetic. But in the process the mathetic/pragmatic opposition has itself disappeared, having created the effective conditions for the emergence of the broad functional components of the adult semantic system. It is largely the mathetic function, that of language as learning, that creates the conditions for the development of ideational meanings, those expressing the speaker's experience of the phenomena around and inside him (processes, quality and quantity, time &c.); and the pragmatic function, that of language as doing, that creates the conditions for the development of interpersonal meanings, those expressing the speaker's role in and angle on the communication process (mood, modality, intensity, &c.). The third component, the text-forming or textual component, evolves during Phase II in the course of the child's construction of narrative and of dialogue. Every utterance in the Phase III language, which is essentially the adult *system*, means, and therefore is structured, in terms of these components simultaneously.

The following section presents in tabular form the details of Nigel's progress through Phase II.

5. NL 6-9: examples

SPECIMENS OF DIALOGUE FROM NL 6 & 7

24 April
    M. Did you tell Daddy what you had for tea? N. (to M., excitedly) aʸì: . . . ò . . . aʸì: aʸì: ('egg, ooh! egg, egg!') yɔylɔywa

('cockadoodledoo'; = cornflakes, because of picture on packet; also = weathercock on church spire, so, having returned from walk, continues with inventory of things seen) tìkə ('and sticks') M. You didn't have cornflakes for tea! N. lɔ̀ᵘ ('and holes') M. You didn't have sticks and holes for tea! N. (returning to the subject in hand) dòuba ('and toast') N. (touching M.'s nose) ⁿdòu ('nose') M. Yes that's my nose. Where's your nose? N. (touching it) dɛ̀ə ('there')

26 April

F. What did you see yesterday? N. kˣà ('car') F. Yes, and you went for a ride in a car, didn't you? and what did you see up there (pointing)? N. tʻà ('tower') F. Yes, you saw a tower. And what did you pick in the garden? N. gɣà ('grass') F. And what else? N. dɛ̀dı ('daisy')

27 April

M. Take the toothpaste to Daddy and go and get your bib. N. dàdā ... nm̄ɔ̀nm̄ɔ̀ ... ʈʉ̀ʈʉ̄ ('Daddy ... noddy (toothpaste) ... (bib with) train (on)')

28 April

M. What is it you can't find? Is it something under there? N. (looking under settee) bɔ̀ ('ball') A. We're going out for a walk, and we'll go and get some fish. N. tìkᵘ ('sticks') A. No, we're not getting any sticks today. N. (plaintively) lɔ̀ᵘ ('holes', = no holes?, what can I put in the holes)?

30 April

N. ádɣ̄dà ('what's that?') F. It's a piece of wood. N. m̀ ('I see!)'
N. ádɣ̄dà ('what's that?') M. That's butter. N. tàbə
N. ɢà:ѡɢà:ѡ ('ducks') F. You saw some ducks. N. tìkᵘ ('sticks') F. And you saw some sticks? N. lɔ̀ᵘ ('holes)' F. And you saw some holes. Did you put the sticks in the holes? N. bà ('buses') F. And you saw some buses. N. dòubā(?) F. You saw some toast and butter? You didn't see any toast and butter! N. dòubā(?) F. (trying again) Two buses? N. (very distinctly and slowly) dōu bà(?) ... ḍɒ̀uə ('tower') F. You saw a tower? N. ḍɒ̀uə ... bì:ˀ ('tower, big') F. You saw a big tower? N. bì:ˀ ('big!') F. Was it the church? (N. is silent: wrong guess) Did you see the church? N. gɔ̄gɫgɔgɫgɔ̀ ('weathercock') F. You saw the weathercock. N. (with music gesture) gɔ̄gɫgɔgɫgɔ̀

89

('sing cockadoodledoo') F. Sing "Cockadoodledoo"? All right.
(F. Sings) N. (with music gesture) bì ('bridge') F. Which is
that one? "London Bridge"? Shall I sing "London Bridge"?
All right.

    A. What will you see when you go out for a walk? N. kà bà
('cars, buses')

    A. What did you see on your walk? N. ᵊbà ᵊkà t'ù ('buses,
cars, trains')

5 May
    N. ɜ̄ ē ɛ̄ ɛ̄ ɛ̄ bʊ̀uwʊ̀u ('hey! dog!':=I want to come and draw
with you (originally='draw dogs')) F. No I'm working. N.
dā:dɪkədà (you're playing the tabla') F. No I'm not playing
dadikeda, I'm writing. N. bʊ̀uwʊ̀u ('then you must be drawing!')

6 May
    N. nēnōnēnɔ̀ ('noddy toothpaste') ɜ̄ ɜ̄ ɜ̄ ɜ̄ ɜ̄ ('I want that') M.
Can you put it (=the top of the tube) on again? N. (soft; high
level, stepping up) ɛ̄ ɛ̄ ('I'll try')
    F. You went on a train yesterday. N. ʧ̩ʧ̩ . . . bā:bā ('train . . .
byebye!';=when I got off, the train went away and I waved to it)
F. And you said "byebye" to the train. N. a:ńfi ('another!')
F. And you saw another train?
    N. (long list of things seen, then:) wlà ('flag') M. Oh you saw
some flags? N. (holding out palm) gɣà ('gravel') M. And you
had some gravel. N. (touching palm, lips rounded, very quiet)
ǫ:=('ooh!') F. And you hurt your hand with the gravel? M.
No, that was with the stick, the one with prickles on. N. blà
('blood') M. And there was blood on it, yes.

7 May
    M. (pointing) Who's that? N. nā ('Anna') M. (pointing
to self) And who's that? N. mā ('Mummy') M. (pointing
to N.) And who's that? N. nī

8 May
    F. Are you going out for a walk? N. dōubà . . . àiʸ ('toast:
eggs':=we're going to buy some bread and some eggs)

9 May
    N. mā ('Mummy!') M. be:ta (=sonny) N. āmā M. be:ja
&c. &c. ad lib.

(NL 2) ɗɔ ɛʸa vɶ   'look, a picture! what is it? a ball!'

(NL 5) dādā dɔ̀u   (daddy toast) 'Daddy's brought some toast'

(NL 6)

1. co-ordinate strings
əbà əkà ʧʉ̀   'buses, cars & trains'
k'àk'àbàbàɢōɢɔ̀   'cars, buses & a weathercock'
kàkàbàbàtìkʷtìkʷlɔ̀ulɔ̀u   'cars, buses, sticks & holes'
tìkᵘtìkᵘlɔ̀ulɔ̀utʉ̀tʉ̀ʧ̣ʉ̀ʧ̣ʉ̀ bɔ̀bɔ̀bàbà   'sticks, holes, stones, trains, balls & buses'
k'àk'àbàbàbàuwàuġɔ̀ġɔ̀ tìkᵘtìkᵘlɔ̀ulɔ̀u   'cars, buses, dogs, a weathercock, sticks & holes'

2. vocalization + gesture
ɛ̀   (do that! + *pick me up) 'pick me up'
ⁿdɔ̀   (star + *negation) 'the star wasn't there any more'
dā:bì   (Dvořak + *music) 'I want the Dvořak record on'

3. general + specific element from same functional category
ʔɔ̀ʔ bɔ̀kəba   (I want! + book) 'I want that book'
ɛ̀ lɔ̀u   (do that! + hole) 'make a hole'
ɔ̀ aʸì: (excitement + egg) 'ooh! an egg'

4. others
dɔ̀bɨ nɔ̀nɔ   (toothbrush, noddy) 'I want my toothbrush & toothpaste'
dɔ̀ə bàuwau   (draw, dog) 'I want to draw—a dog'
lɛ̀la dà   (letter, there) 'the letters—there they are'
bʌbʷɔ̀ nɔ̄ᵘmɔ̀   (bubble, no-more) 'the bubbles have gone away'
tīkə lɔ̀uba   (stick, hole) 'I'll put my stick in the hole(?)'

*=gesture

(NL 7)

1. co-ordinate strings: frequent, e.g.
   tìkᶜᵒtìkᶜᵒlɔ̀ulɔ̀udə̀də̀kˣàkˣà   'sticks, holes, trains, cars, buses
   bàbàbàuwàu   & dogs'

2. vocalization + gesture
   lì ɸọ   (leaf + *blowing) 'the leaves
                                           are blowing in the wind'

3. general + specific element from same functional category
   nɔ̀:bənɒ: ... ē ... mā ...   (banana + I want + mummy)
   əmmā   'I want Mummy's banana'

Structures from 28 May—3 June:

28 v	1	àdʒɐ ... þʸà:o ... à:ɷ	(Andrew, piano, house) 'Andrew plays the piano in his house'; or 'Andrew plays the piano; so did I, in Anna's house'
	2	āpì ... dàda ... āmà ... ān:à	(apple, daddy, mummy, Anna) 'I've got an apple; so has Daddy; so has Mummy; so has Anna'
	3	dɔ̀bɪ ... dá:dɔ̀bɪ	'a toothpick, a tiny toothpick'
29 v	4	bɹkɛ̀ ... ōdɪɔ̀ ... mì? ... dàda	(breakfast, oh-dear!, milk, daddy) 'I want my breakfast—I'm hungr!y—milk! and some for Daddy too'
30 v	5	tʃɔ̀ʸa ... là ... gɹì ... lagɹɪ	(train, light, green; light green) 'the train went and the light turned green'
31 v	6	gɹì: ... gɹ̄ī: là	'green, a green light'
	7	dâ ... dā: dɔ̀:bɪ	'tiny—a tiny toothpick'
	8	gɹ̄ī:kà	'a green car'
	9	əloᶜᵒ tí:ko:	'hullo teacosy!'
1 vi	10	gɹ:ī: kà ... bl:ū:kà ... aǹʰ:	(green car, blue car, another) 'I saw a green car, and a blue car, and lots more'

	11	mɔ̄: mìˀ	'more meat!'
	12	mɔ̄: mìˀ plɪ	'more meat please!'
		tʉ̄ bɷ̀kʷ	'two books'
2 vi	14	tʉ̄ ɛ̀kl̩	'two helicopters' (also two + various other things'
	15	gɹɪ̄: là	'green light' (also green car)
3 vi	16	mɔ̄: ɔ̀blə	'more omelet'
	17	gɹɪ̄: pɛ̀ˀ	'green peg'

NL 7 (18–19½ months): PRAGMATIC & MATHETIC

PRAGMATIC (= Phase I: Instrumental, Regulatory, some Interactional); tone changes to rising

'I want':

dèbɪ	toothpaste	ɹ̩̀gɔ	cotton-reel	to end of May: all falling tone
mᵇɪ̀	milk	vòb̥a	fish	
bɷ̀	bone	gà:ɔbʷga:ɔ	cardamum	
nōumɔ̀		'(there's) no more'		
ōdì:ə		'sing "Oh dear what can the matter be"'		
bɹ̩̀ . . . nò . . . dàlon		'don't sing "London Bridge", sing "The cheese stands alone"'		

kɐ̄m	'come with me'	very narrow falling tone	first week in June: transitional
ˀɔ̄fvə	'take it off'		
dʸkā	'get down'		
dɒ̄u	'sit down'		
ōɹʷɪ̄ kɐ̄m	'I want my orange'	(level tone)	

'I want':

bɔ́l̥	ball	báu	to bounce	Second week in June onwards: all rising tone
bɹɛ́kə	breakfast	mɔ̄bɹɛ́	more bread	
kɐ́m		'come with me'		
āgǽi		'do it again'		
ɔ̄ᵘvᵊdɛ́ə		'come over there'		
dɒ́u		'sit down'		
mɐ̄mɪ̄ kɐ́m		'mummy come'		
nó		'no (I don't want)'		
bɐ̄tɐ̄ ˀɔ́n		'put some butter on'		
kwɪ̄: ˀɔɹ́ʷɪ		'squeeze the orange'		

nᴅʊ ɹʊ́m	'now (let's go to Daddy's) room'	Second
mɛn ʧʊ́va	'mend the train'	week in June
dā: vɔ́ja	'(draw a) star for you (=for me)'	onwards: all rising
ɛpĺ . . . ɛpĺ tʉ́	'help . . . help (me with the) juice'	tone
kēm ōᵘvᵊdɛ́ə	'come over there'	
bī:gᵊ bʊ́kʊwa	'I want my big book'	

MATHETIC (=Phase I: some Interactional, Personal, Heuristic); all falling tone

Observation and recall/things:

ɹɛ̄: kà	red car	bl̞ū bɔ̀l̞	blue ball	
ɹɛ̄: bɹɛ̀la	red umbrella	blu̞ū kwɛ̀ə	blue square	
gɹī: tɔ̀wəl	green towel	vā: ʧɔ̀va	fast train	
bī ʔ tòn	big stone	bī:gᵊ bɔ̀k	big book	
t'ʉ̄ àpa	two apples	mēmī bɔ̀kᵊ	Mummy's book	

gɹī ol̞ ʧɔ̀va	green old train
tʉ̄ vā: ʧɔ̀va	two fast trains
dā: ɹʷɛ̄ là	tiny red light

Observation and recall—processes:

bī: bī: làwa	'bee on the flower'
vò tɛ̀ ʔ	'foot stuck'
bēbʷ ɹᴅuɹᴅu	'bubbles (go) round and round'
vòpa . . . ɔpēn mᴅu	'fishes opening their mouths'

Narrative:

tᴅʊ tʃɔ̀va . . . lɛ̄ bɹì	(we went to) town (on a) train, to London Bridge
tɹì . . . ʔɔ́ . . . tìkawɛ̀: . . . ōḡɔ̀ . . . bābā	tree broken, take away, all gone, byebye!
gɹī: tìk . . . lɔ̀tᶜᵊ . . . gɔ̀n: . . . bāʸbāʸ	green stick, lost, gone, byebye!
blā ʔ miào . . . ɹʷā dɔ̀ᵊ	black cat, (it) ran indoors

Narrative with quoted speech:

qàɪ . . . qàɪ . . . maɪ̄nn̞ tìŋ	(there was a) kite; (Daddy said, "there's a) kite; mind the string"

Structures of one and two elements: all rising tone unless otherwise noted

where dàddy	N. out with Anna, met Fąther unexpectedly; sense 'look there's Daddy!'—(falling tone)
chuffa stúck	N. calling for help in freeing toy train
find fóryou	'I've lost something; find it for me!'
throw úp	'throw the rabbit up in the air again'
low wáll	N. about to jump off suitcase, asking to be
high wáll	caught; first used when jumping off walls, low & high, in park
squéeze	'squeeze the orange for me'
gláss	'I want my milk in a glass'
orange lèmon	'sing "Oranges and lemons"'; accompanied by music gesture, which is alternative realization of pragmatic; hence falling tone
turn róund	N. repeating instruction given when fitting shapes into puzzles: 'is that what I have to do?'
play chúffa	'let's play with the train'
open fóryou	(usual form of request for box, &c., to be opened)
back tóothpaste	'put the toothpaste back in the cupboard'
more grávy	also: more ómelet, -léttuce, -tomáto, -bréad, -bún, &c.
bounce táble	'I want to bounce my orange on the table'
cárry	'carry me!'
háve it	(usual form of 'I want that thing')
tóast	'I want some toast'; also breakfast, tomato &c.
hit flóor	'I'm going to hit the floor with the hammer'
that sóng	'sing that song you've just sung'
háve that	(same as have it above)
hedgehog bóok	'I want the book with the hedgehog picture in it'
play ráo	'I want to play at lions'

Note: Up to the first week of July (i.e. half way through NL 8,
which covers the period mid June to end July), two-element
structures predominate; the above examples are taken from

throughout NL 8 but mainly from the earlier part. After the first week in July there is a predominance of structures of three or more elements; those in the next list are taken mainly from the later part of NL 8.

NL 8: PRAGMATIC

Structures of three & more elements; all rising tone unless otherwise noted

toothpaste ón ... red tòothbrush	'put the toothpaste on the red toothbrush'; pause for planning 2nd half
train under túnnel ... getit fóryou	both halves rising tone
dówn ... table ... sugar ... spóon	'put the sugar down on the table for me to put my spoon it it'; rising tone on down and spoon
make cross tíckmatick ... in dada róom	'I want to make crosses on the typewriter in Daddy's room'; both halves rising tone
réd train might break	following that blue train might break; earliest utterance interpretable as a yes/no question
get stick báll	'I want the stick to get the ball with'; also: get ball stíck
bounce big báll	
dada get off coathanger fóryou	'Daddy take the coathanger off for me'
dada squeeze out toothpaste fóryou	
anna help gréenpea	'Anna help me to eat the green peas'
big bubble gòne ... big búbble ... móre big bubble	'the big bubble's burst; I want another one'
butter on knífe	'I want—'
take marmite kítchen	'can I—?'
anna put record on fóryou	
that go thére	'will that go there?'
go abbeywood on tráin	'let's go to Abbey Wood on the train'
have tóothpowder ... nila have tóoth powder	

96

play highwall mátchstick	'let me jump holding the matchstick'
dada put alltogéther egg	'Daddy put the eggs all together (one inside the other)'
when newworld fĭnish song about bús	'when New World finishes (falling tone), sing me the song about the bus (rising)'

Dialogues involving pragmatic utterances

F. D'you want the black brush? N. nó F. D'you want the
black and the red brush? N. yés
  F. Mummy's gone to the shop. N. buy chócolate
  N. put bemax down on táble M. It is on the table. N.
nĭla table
  N. why that clóck stop F. I don't know: why do you think?
N. ménd it

NL 8 (19½–21 months): (2) MATHETIC

Structures of one & two elements; all falling tone

molasses nòse	'I've got molasses on my nose' (with accompanying expression of delight)
big bàll	frequent when playing with ball; also: little bàll
mummy bòok	frequent on picking up book and finding no pictures inside ('it's Mummy's book')
red swèater	on seeing it; also: red jùmper (same object)
black brùsh	also green, red, blue, yellow with stick, light, peg, car, train &c.
bìg one	applied to goods train, bubble; tonic on big, as in adult form
baby dùck	in picture; also: mummy dùck
too bìg	frequent; sometimes appropriate, as when trying to push object through wire mesh; sometimes inappropriate, as when trying to reach ball with stick (='too far')
that bròke	'that's broken'
loud mùsic	frequent comment as loud passage starts
chuffa stòp	in game (Father bouncing N., N. being 'fast train'; Father stops)

Note: There is also considerable use of single words as holophrases
in contexts of observation and recall, e.g. fire, chocolate, feather,

rhinoceros, bee, cherry. This phenomenon is noticeably less frequent with familiar than with unfamiliar words.

Both one- and two- element utterances become relatively less frequent during the second half of this period. The examples in the next list are typical of the longer utterances that characterize the latter part of NL 8.

Structures of three & four elements; all falling tone except where otherwise indicated

two green pèg	
green stick fĩnd	'the green stick's been found'
old green tràin . . . green old tràiŋ	both halves falling tone; the second, though less probable, would have been the appropriate one in the context
dada black brùsh	'Daddy's black brush'
no more wàter	
toothpaste . . . òn . . . tòothbrush	falling tone <u>on</u> on and again on <u>toothbrush</u>; not fully formed as a single structure
tree fall dòwn	later: big tree fall dòwn
dada got bàll . . . nila got bàll	
ball go under càr	cf. water gone plùghole
one blúe train . . . one rèd train	tone and tonicity as in adult language (i.e. rising tonic on <u>blue</u>, falling tonic on <u>red</u>)
glass got hòle	looking at glass with pattern of bubbles
that blue train might brèak	
dada come bàck . . . dada come on fast tràin	
man clean càr	'there's a man cleaning a car'
very old trèe	
nila get dada tìn	'Nigel & Daddy will get the tin' (sic)
anna got piano anna hòuse . . . very òld one . . . (shaking head) very gòod one	(routine) 'Anna's got a piano at home, a very old one, not a very good one'

anna make noise gràss	'Anna made a noise with the grass';
... that not right	second half imitation of what Anna
kìnd grass	had said
strange man gòne	
red egg hòt	(plastic egg in basin of hot water)
clever boy fix roof on	
lòrry	
too dark ... open cùr-	'it was too dark; the curtains have
tain ... lìght now	been opened, and now it's light'
have clare banàna	'Clare had a banana'
letter fall out mummy	
bòok	

Dialogues and strings involving mathetic utterances

N. (holding one train and one bus) two ... two chùffa ... two ... two (puzzled; gives up)

N. two fast chùffa   M. Where did you see two fast trains?
N. wàlk   M. And what else did you see?   N. bòwwow

N. dada got scrambled ègg ... mummy get fóryou scrambled egg (second half has rising tonic on foryou, marking shift to pragmatic function 'I want,' with scrambled egg as 'given' element.

N. (getting off train) train go cròss (=Charing Cross) ... go tòwn ... no more tràin ... time go hòme ... have òrange ... squeeze òrange

N. bird on wàll ... wàlking ... tiny bird flew awày.   F. Did it?
N. ōhyēs

N. big nòise   M. Who made a big noise?   N. drìll make big noise

N. bùmblebee   M. Where was the bumblebee?   N. bumble-bee on tràin   M. What did Mummy do?   N. mummy open wìndow   M. Where did the bumblebee go?   N. bumblebee flew awày

N. (pointing) got nòse ... dada got nòse ... mùmmy got nose ... ànna got nose

NL 9 (21–22½ months)

Examples in chronological sequence

N. dear dèar ... chuffa fall òver ... big bàng

N. what élse put in ('what else can I put into the water?')

A. Shall we go for a walk?   N. when E-I-O fìnish (song on record)

99

N. why brόken that ('why is that broken?')

N. Pauline went on two fast chùffa ... one fast chuffa hére ...
one chuffa ... one fast chuffa brìdge ('one·here and oné at London
Bridge')

N. record back on ráck ... new record back on ráck ... what
élse put on ... what élse put on ('put the new record back on the
rack and put something else on!')

N. Oh dear dear dèar ... lorry fell òver ... on ... thàt (piece
of furniture of which he does not know the name)

N. flỳ ... flỳ ... climbing up tàble ... climbing mummy chàir
... fly clìmbing

M. (looking for lost toy) I can't find the driver's head. N. gone
under bèd ... háve it (3) ... ooh dear dèar ... háve it

N. (playing with toy cow) cow eat gráss ('let me make the cow
eat grass')

N. dada get knife take skin off ápple (request)

N. eat chúffa F. You can't eat trains! N. can't eat blue
chùffa F. No you can't eat the blue train. N. can't eat rèd
chuffa F. No you can't eat the red train. N. (looking at
wooden man from toy cart) can't eat màn F. No you can't eat
the man. N. can't eat that bòok F. No you can't eat that
book! you can't eat any book. N. (looking at Pauline) can't eat
Pàuline book. F. No you can't eat Pauline's book. N. Pauline
got èar F. (moving Pauline's hair aside) Yes Pauline's got an ear,
though you can't usually see it. N. dàda got ear ... dada got
nòse F. Yes. N. (touching Pinocchio doll) Pinocchio got funny
nòse F. Yes Pinocchio's got a funny nose, like a— N. càrrot
F. Yes like a carrot. N. scrèwdriver ... mend Pinocchio fòot
(reference to F.'s mending Pinocchio's foot some days earlier)

N. (to F., who has finished shaving, is putting shirt on) put
that όn (2) ... dada ready nòw (4) ... put that όn ... dada ready
nόw (4)

N. (looking at opening in top of packet of Bemax, inside outer
cover) hole in bèmax ... (closing outer cover, so that hole is
concealed) where hόle

N. (beating time with chopsticks) condùctor ('I'm being a
conductor')

F. (on station platform) There are people on the platform.
N. waiting chuffa còme

N. chuffa walk on ràilway line (2) ... fast chùffa ... one day
might gò on fast chuffa (2) F. Yes we might. N. one day go on
blue chùffa ... next chuffa còming ... go on thàt one

N. (looking at pictures) umbrèlla ... bòat ... stìck ... twèet-tweet ... bòwwow

A. Can I brush your hair Nigel? N. nó ... nó

N. lunch back on táble ('I don't want any more')

N. (F. is holding pin in mouth) dada put pin in my mòuth
F. No, not in Nigel's mouth; in Daddy's mouth. N. not in nìla mouth ... dada put pin in mòuth

N. (being put to bed) didn't clean your tèeth ('I didn't clean my teeth!')

F. Did you walk on the platform? N. walk on ràilway line
F. I don't think you did! N. walk on plàtform ... not walk on ràilway line (routine)

M. Where do the cars go? N. on ròad M. And where do the trains go? N. on ràilway line M. And where does Nigel go? N. on ràilway line (routine)

N. (knocks on F.'s door; F. opens) téatime ... lúnchtime ... nila take lunch on táble ('shall I take my lunch on the table?')

A. What did the baby have in the pram? N. blànket ... not yòur blanket ... bàby blanket ... (pointing to his room) your blanket thère

N. that very hòt ('that pan is very hot') ... thát very hot ('is that handle very hot?')

N. (trying to stand F.'s book up on end) look at dada bóok ... stand úp ... stand úp F. No it won't stand up. (it did) N. clever bòy

N. dada brùsh ... play dada brúsh ... hôle ... got hòle in it (repet.) ... hole in tòothbrush ... hole in dada tòothbrush (delight)

N. play rao bártok ('I want to play at lions with me holding the sleeve of the Bartok record')

N. anna say go awày nila ('Anna said "go away Nigel"')

N. when music fińish then I sing you dùck song ('when this music's finished you're going to sing me the duck song, aren't you?')

F. (playing lions) This is an eat train lion. N. (picks up engine and gives it to F. to eat)

N. I go shòpping A. Are you going shopping? What are you going to buy? N. ègg A. Where do you buy eggs from? N. Madeline Mòore (The answer is appropriate. It is doubtful whether N.'s first utterance was intended as pretend-play; possibly = 'you're going shopping'.)

F. After breakfast where are we going, do you know? N. àbbeywood F. No not Abbey Wood. N. ólly ('are we going to see Olly?')

N. (at station) chuffa go in mòment ... that chuffa go in mòment ... another chuffa hère ... that train gòing ... that train staying hère ... people want get òff that train   M. What a lot of trains!   N. two chùffa ... can't see drìver ... can't see drìver in that one

N. (having fallen earlier in the day, touching forehead) ády̅dà ('what's that?')   F. That's plaster, sticking plaster   N. tell mummy take it òff ... (running to M.) take it óff

N. that tree got no lèaf on ... stick ('it's all made of sticks') ... thát tree got leaf on but that tree got no lèaf on

N. (finding strand of M.'s hair and stretching it out straight) mummy hair like ràilway line

N. have céllo ('I want the record sleeve with the picture of the cello on')   Grandmother. Does he know what a cello looks like?   F. I don't think he's ever seen a cello.   N. have seen cello in pàrk (in fact he hasn't, but he has often seen brass bands playing in park.)

N. have blue pin all ríght ('I can, can't I?')   M. The blue pin has got lost.   N. under béd   M. No it's not under the bed.   N. blue pin got lòst ... whíte pin got lost   M. No the white pin didn't get lost.   N. (pricking pin into vest) that white pin prick your tùmmy ... that white pin prick your knèe ... (sticking it into bedcover) make hòle

N. have nellie élephant bib   M. Nellie the elephant bib's being washed; it may not be dry yet.   N. have chúffa bib (goes out to look for it; brings back cat bib) ... that not chuffa bib that miào bib ... put miao bib ón

N. (hearing vacuum cleaner) r̀-r̀-r̀   M. What's making that noise?   N. chùffa   M. No it's not a train.   N. àeroplane   M. No its not an aeroplane.   N. càr   N. No it's not a car.   N. clèaner   M. Yes that's right. (All very serious—apparently a genuine search.)

6. Interpretation of Phase II

I. PRAGMATIC

Pragmatic contexts are those which evolve out of the instrumental and regulatory functions of Phase I. At the beginning of Phase I, the instrumental take the form of requests for food, for entertainment (music), and for objects as symbols—that is, objects other than his own possessions (which tend not to be explicitly demanded, though it should be remembered that the generalized demand forms of the earlier phase, 'give me that!', remain in use well into Phase II) that are a focus of personal identification or ritual interaction—father's keys, mother's lipstick, certain books, and the like. As Nigel's semantic potential increases, this component expands into a general realm of 'goods and services'. The regulatory meanings now extend across the three modes of the adult imperative, first person 'let me', i.e. 'I'm going to', second person 'you!', and first and second person 'let's'. These include specific demands for assistance, for movement (places and postures), for objects to be manipulated and so on. There is a close functional relationship among all of these, which we are expressing by the use of the term 'pragmatic', and which Nigel is soon to make explicit by the rising intonation pattern; and also between these and certain meanings deriving from the interactional function—those concerned with the search for other people and the demand for a response from them.

The significant feature that emerges is the steadily increasing content that is associated with pragmatic utterances. The child's requirements can no longer be formulated in terms merely of objects or actions, involving the simple semantic relation of 'object of desire'. They have to be expressed in complex patterns, semantic configurations in which the desired object or service is garnished in some way, for example with the meaning 'more' (more méat) or by reference to some relation or process (Bartok ón, squeeze órange), including processes which relate the object to himself (help júice). If the request is for an action, this comes to involve specification of the kind of action by means of an element expressing the Range (play tráin, play líons), or by the addition of circumstantial elements (bounce táble, i.e. 'I want to bounce my orange on the table'); and including instances where only the circumstances are specified, the action being left unsaid (now róom, i.e. 'now let's go to (play in) your room'). Furthermore the request may be encoded as a statement of an undesired condition to be relieved (train stúck, train under túnnel). These elements soon come to be combined, so that by NL 8 we get complex request forms such as make cross tíckmatick . . . in dada róom ('I want to make a cross on the typewriter, in Daddy's room') and when newworld fínish song about bús ('when New World finishes sing me the bus song').

This last request shows for the first time a true integration of the two modes of meaning; and it is one in which the mathetic is operating as a circumstantial qualification of the pragmatic. Hence it happens that the tonal pattern is exactly the reverse of that of the adult language, which typically would have a rise on the first part, signalling its dependence, and a fall on the second, the typical form of the imperative: When the New World fínishes, sing me the song about a bùs. But the general significance of the increasing content that comes to be associated with pragmatic utterances is the interactive one: the semantic system is constructed in the process of interaction. The pragmatic mode of meaning, language in action, creates the need for complex semantic configurations; while the effective response to the demands which these express creates the conditions for their continued expression and expansion.

The pragmatic component is the source of the mood system of the adult language. Here we find not only the prototype for the various forms of the imperative mentioned above, but also the origin of questions, which with Nigel seems to lie particularly in the context of trial and error in the manipulation of objects, e.g. that go thére 'does that go there?', that blue train might brèak . . . réd train might break 'you told me the blue train might break; now tell me whether the red train might break'. The mood system is an interactive one; in fact it is the semantics of linguistic inter-action—a question seeks a response, and once the question has evolved to include 'true' questions, searches for information as distinct from requests, the response typically takes the form of a statement—and this, in turn, in the terms of the pragmatic/mathetic opposition, is mathetic in function, though it is an extension of the mathetic as originally defined, which did not include giving information. True questions of this kind appear in the second h.lf of Phase II, and provide the condition for the shift in the mode of response. Until this time, the typical response to a pragmatic utterance is non-verbal: it is an action, even if that action is accompanied by some verbal signal of accession to the request. So when Nigel says play chúffa 'let's play trains', there may be a verbal response to the interpersonal component of the meaning (to the imperative mood) in the form of 'yes let's, shall we? all right' and such like; but the response to the ideational component of the meaning (the content of the request) takes the form of action—the addressee does what the child asks. (He may refuse to do it, of course, but this does not affect the argument). But if the question is a search for information, the response is entirely verbal: not only the interpersonal component 'yes I will answer your question', which now does not need to be verbalized (since the act of responding is performative in this respect) although it often is, typically by the word 'well' at the beginning of the answer, but also the ideational component which now takes the form of information —the addressee tells what the child wants to know. From the child's point of view, of course, this is turning the developmental process back to front. What the child does is to derive from the semiotic system that he has created for other purposes—not only pragmatic purposes, as we have emphasized, but certainly excluding any conception of an informative function—the concept of information that is inherent in it. A symbolic system that serves to encode other, non-symbolic meanings can also create symbolic meanings of its own, those of 'telling' and 'asking'. (No doubt this is learnt, in part, through the various types of non-responses to requests, disclaimers of various kinds which have to be verbal; for example 'it is on the table' in the sequence: N. put bemax on táble   M. It is on the table.   N. nígel table.) Through this route the child comes to master what was the last in the original list of developmental functions, the 'informative' function. The use of language to inform is, as we have repeatedly pointed out, a highly complex notion. All the other functions, whether active or reflective— whether concerned with exploiting the environment or with interpreting it — are independent of language; language intervenes as a symbolic means to an end that is defined in non-linguistic terms. But telling and asking are themselves symbolic acts. The use of language to inform depends on conceptualizing the fact that, once the semiotic system has been evolved, it creates its own meanings; the exchange of symbols becomes a function in its own right. All parents are familiar with the typical Phase II sequence of events in which, after the child has shared some interesting experience with his mother, she invites him to 'tell Granny what happened'. The child is tongue-tied. He is perfectly capable of verbalizing the experience, and may even turn to his mother and do so; but he has not yet learnt that language is not just an *expression* of shared experience, it is an *alternative* to it, a means of imparting the experience to the other. For the same reason, when he first learns to anwer a WH-question, he can do so only if he knows that the answer is already known to the person who is asking the question. It is only towards the end of Phase II that Nigel grasps this principle; and when he does, he continues for many months to draw a clear semantic distinction between telling people what they already know (verbalizing shared experience), for which he uses the (unmarked) declarative mood, and telling people what they do not know (verbalizing as a means of sharing experience), for which he uses the (marked) interrogative mood.

2. MATHETIC
Meanwhile he has developed to a high degree language in its mathetic function, the use of the symbolic system not as a means of acting on reality but as a means of learning about reality. This is the primary context for the evolution of the ideational systems of the adult language: classes of objects, quality and quantity, transitivity and the like. The context in which these systems evolve is that of the observation of how things are. Nigel's experience of how things are is such that it can be represented in terms of processes, of people and things functioning as participants in these processes, and of accompanying circumstances. Not that reality can *only* be represented in this way, but this is a *possible* semantic interpretation; the fact that Nigel adopts this form of representation rather than another one is because this is the way it is done in the language he hears around him. We readily assume that the semiotics of social interaction—the interpersonal component of the semantic system—is constructed in the course of interaction; but it is no less true that the construction of a semiotic of reality— the ideational component—is also an interactive process. Nigel soon begins to use dialogue as a means of building up complex representations; for example (NL 9)   F. There are people on the platform.   N. Waiting chuffa còme. (Compare the many instances of the building up of description and narrative by means of question and answer.)

Nigel goes into Phase II with a set of words for objects, thing names which are used in observation, recall and prediction; together with a negative which may accompany them in the sense of 'no longer there', and which is expressed by gesture (a shake of the head—it is a long time before he has a verbalized negative in the mathetic mode). The classes of objects are, at first, things in pictures, things seen on walks, small household objects, parts of the body and items of food (the latter being largely different from those found in the pragmatic context, since not valued as items for his own consumption). Then the horizons begin to broaden, first through the introduction of names of properties accompanying the object names; the first to appear are colours and the number two (green càr, two pèg). Next circumstantial elements are introduced, typically expressions of place (as with other structures, these are built up step by step, first as semantic constructs and later grammaticalized: <u>toothpaste òn</u> . . . <u>tòothbrush</u> before <u>ball go under càr</u>). Next come complex processes involving two elements besides the process itself: either two participants, or a participant and a circumstance. By NL 8 Nigel's world extends to complex phenomena such as <u>dada come on fast tràin</u> and <u>anna make noise gràss.</u>

All these elements, and their combinations, tend to appear in a mathetic context before they appear in a pragmatic one, which is what we might expect. But there is an interesting exception, and one that is right at the heart of the system. The processes themselves—words that will turn into verbs—often appear first in a pragmatic context; and this is particularly true of those that introduce the ergative (causational) element in the semantic system. By and large, Nigel's early process-participant combinations, those that will turn into verb + noun, have the participant as 'Medium'—in terms of the adult language, intransitive Actor or transitive Goal. These may appear in either context: 'things happen' or 'I want things to happen'. Soon, however, he introduces agentive constructs; and here the mediating function seems to be the pragmatic one, the meaning being 'let *me* cause things to happen' (<u>look at dada bóok</u> . . . stand úp . . . stand úp 'I am going to stand it up'). Without making too much of this—the evidence is slender—we can suggest that perhaps the pragmatic function contributes to the development of transitivity specifically by creating the conditions for the representation of the causative element in the structure of processes; there is an echo here of Phase I regulatory meanings, where 'do that again!' meant 'make it jump', and of early Phase II demands such as bounce meaning 'bounce the ball' or 'bounce me'.

Be that as it may, the general pattern seems to be that the pragmatic function of Phase II creates the conditions for the development of the interpersonal component in the adult semantic system, and the mathetic function creates the conditions for the ideational component. This, essentially, is why the adult language has evolved in the way it has done: it meets the twofold needs of acting on the environment and reflecting on it (the latter, in a developmental context, being interpretable as learning about it). If we have tended to make a great point of this parallel development, it is because there are two mainstream traditions in the interpretation of child language, each emphasizing one component to the exclusion of the other. One tradition derives from cognitive psychology, and assumes that the only function of language is ideational: if the child learns to talk, this is simply to express ideas, and ideas are about things and their relations. The other derives from social anthropology, and assumes that the real function of language is interpersonal: the child learns to talk in order to get what he wants, which means getting other people (or spirits) to give it to him, or do it for him. Obviously, both of these are essential parts of the picture. (So also, we might add, is a third, minor tradition, probably deriving from aesthetics, according to which the child learns language in order to sing and play.) The real interest lies in seeing *how* these functions determine the ontogeny of the system, and how they interpenetrate at various key points in the developmental process.

3. BREAKDOWN OF THE PRAGMATIC/MATHETIC SYSTEM

Each function, we are suggesting, carries with it a strong sub-motif of the other. Pragmatic utterances also concern things and their relations, and some aspects of these—such as, if we are right, the causative element in processes—may actually be verbalized first in a pragmatic context. Similarly, mathetic utterances also involve some kind of a stance vis-a-vis the environment; the sort of intensification and evaluation that appear in very old trèe, loud nòise, big bàng and expressions with too—too is particularly complex, since it is an evaluative element interpretable in terms only of some reference point, and this reference point may be the speaker's opinion. All these appear first in mathetic contexts.

But the point has to be made in more general terms. When we say that the mathetic function creates the conditions for the emergence of the ideational component in the semantic system, and the pragmatic for the interpersonal component, this means that the ideational systems—transitivity (types of process, participants, circumstances), lexical taxonomy (hierarchy of thing names), quality and quantity &c.—evolve first and foremost in mathetic contexts, while the interpersonal systems—mood (indicative, declarative and interrogative, imperative), modality, person, intensity, comment &c.—evolve first and foremost in pragmatic contexts. We are referring, of course, to these systems in the child's developing semantics; his mood system is very different from that of the adult language, and it is a long time before either the system or its grammatical manifestations take the adult form. What we are describing is the evolution of the concept of function, from its Phase II sense of 'generalized context of language use' to its Phase III sense of 'component of the semantic system'.

But if we then look back at Phase II from the standpoint of the organization of the Phase III system, we can see that this organization is present in prototypic form from the start. In Phase II terms, each utterance is either pragmatic or mathetic; this is attested in Nigel's phonology, in which everything must be either rising or falling tone; and it is the form of continuity from the functional meanings of his Phase I system, each of which is specific and simple—one meaning, in one function, at a time. In Phase III terms, however, all utterances are both ideational and interpersonal at the same time; and this is true—inescapably—from the moment the child builds a lexicogrammar into the system. As soon as the utterance consists of words-in-structure, it has an ideational meaning—a content, in terms of the child's experience; and an interpersonal meaning—an interactional role in the speech situation. (The choice between mathetic and pragmatic is itself an interpersonal system, since it encodes the semiotic role the child is adopting for himself and assigning to the hearer.) This is what we mean by saying that Phase II is transitional. It is not so much a system in its own right, intermediate between baby language and adult language, but rather a period of overlap between the two. The interpretation in terms of the 'Phase II functions', pragmatic and mathetic, an opposition that turns up frequently under different names in language development studies, is one way of explaining the nature of this overlap; but it is also more than that—it is actually Nigel's major strategy for making the transition, as shown by the fact that he clearly assigns every utterance to one mode or the other.

The direction of eventual breakdown of this opposition, as the meaning it expresses evolves and becomes absorbed into the adult mood system, can be seen in two distinct though related processes from about the middle of Phase II onwards. These are the two ways in which mathetic and pragmatic may combine with each other, one linear the other simultaneous. On the one hand, it becomes increasingly common for an utterance to be formed out of a mathetic and a pragmatic component in succession; they may occur in either sequence and, before long, more than one of either may be present. This happens first through changes in the context of the utterance; for example, N. (to F.) tell mummy take it òff ('I'm going to . . .') . . . (running to M.) take it óff. But it soon extends beyond this to sequences in which he simply switches from one meaning to the other: dada got scrambled ègg . . . mummy get fóryou scrambled egg 'Daddy's got some; now get some for me'; and from this it is a short step to complex utterances in which one becomes a condition on the other: when newworld fĩnish song about bús, referred to above. By the end of NL 9 the intonation of these begins to change: when music ffínish then I sing you dùck song. This is the first sign of the breakdown of the rising/falling opposition, perhaps here under strong pressure from the adult system (which in just this context is directly the converse of his own), though it continues to determine the system for some months to come.

On the other hand, it becomes increasingly clear that, while any given utterance or portion of an utterance continues to be explicitly signalled as pragmatic or mathetic, what this expresses is the dominant mode rather than the exclusive mode. It no longer makes sense to interpret the utterances as having meaning exclusively in respect of one function; the function that is assigned (by intonation) is rather the key signature, or prevailing mode for interpretation (cf. 'mood' in the adult system). So when Nigel says, coming into father's study, téatime . . . lúnchtime, there is obviously an observational ('mathetic') element in the meaning: 'it's teatime—I mean it's lunchtime'; what the selection of pragmatic does is to embed this in a context of action, showing that its real significance is as an instruction 'so come along!'—as is made very clear by the follow-up nila take lunch on táble. Similarly there is a pragmatic element in the meaning of dada ready nòw 'Daddy's ready now—at least I want him to be', as seen from the fact that, on finding that Daddy was not in fact ready, he repeats the same sentence on a rising tone: dada ready nów ('please!').

So by the time the pragmatic/mathetic intonation system does break down, as it has to do in Phase III in order to allow the rising/falling contrast to carry the meanings it has in the adult system, it no longer fits in with Nigel's semantic potential. It is unnecessary, because its role has been taken over by the mood system; and it is also inappropriate, because it imposes a dominance of one mode over the other. The supreme quality of human language is that every semiotic act is a blend of action and reflection. This is what we mean by saying that all utterances are structured on both the ideational and the interpersonal dimensions simultaneously. In order to reach this point, the child has to go through an 'either/or' stage in which each utterance means on one dimension only, as he gradually builds the edifice that allows him to combine them. The functional framework, which has served as the scaffolding, now becomes an obstruction and is dismantled.

4. TEXTURE

Meanwhile, in the course of Phase II, and as part of the same general process, Nigel has introduced texture into the system. In terms of the adult language, this represents the third, 'text-forming' component of meaning: it is the potential the system has for being operational in a context, and therefore it is an enabling condition on the other two components—without texture, 'meaning' is a meaningless activity. Texture implies genre, a mode of organization of meaning that relates to function in the other sense of the term that we have now separated off from function interpreted as 'metafunction'—that is, it relates to function in the sense of use: to social context, or situation type. The texture of discourse depends not only on structuring the parts in an appropriate way and joining them together, but on doing so in a way that relates to the context—as narrative, as dialogue, or whatever generic mode is selected.

In Phase II Nigel recognizes two generic structures: narrative, and dialogue. Narrative involves entirely mathetic sequences; dialogue is mixed, but often has a strongly pragmatic component. The two are not, of course, pure categories; narratives occur in dialogue settings, and dialogue is used as a means of constructing narrative. But each has its characteristic forms of organization. Question and answer, for example, is a form of texture that belongs to dialogue, whereas sequences of observations typically occur in narrative. As we saw in Chapter 4, Nigel starts early in Phase II forming sequences that have a semantic structure but not yet a grammatical structure, like 'tree, broken, take-away, all-gone, byebye'; these are early narratives. As time goes on, he learns to represent sequences such as these in a grammatically structured form; but meanwhile his semantic structures have themselves become more complex, so that they are beyond the range of grammatical structure but are structured in the generic sense—they have texture as narrative.

An interesting feature of such sequences is how they are built up through dialogue. The following is an example. Nigel, at 20 months, has been taken to the zoo, and in the children's section has picked up a plastic lid which he is clutching in one hand while stroking a goat with the other. The goat, after the manner of its kind, starts to eat the lid. The keeper intervenes, and says kindly but firmly that the goat must not eat the lid—it would not be good for it. Here is Nigel reviewing the incident after returning home, some hours later:

N. try eat l̀id
F. What tried to eat the lid?
N. try eat l̀id
F. What tried to eat the lid?
N. g̀oat ... man said nò ... goat try eat l̀id ... man said nò

Then, after a further interval, while being put to bed:

N. goat try eat l̀id ... man said nò
M. Why did the man say no?
N. goat sh̀ouldn't eat lid ... (shaking head) g̀oodfor it
M. The goat shouldn't eat the lid; it's not good for it.
N. goat try eat l̀id ... man said nò ... goat sh̀ouldn't eat lid ...
(shaking head) g̀oodfor it

This story is then repeated as a whole, verbatim, at frequent intervals over the next few months.

The outcome of the dialogue is a typical narrative sequence, a set of utterances that are related as parts of a narrative. But as well as having this 'generic' structure, they also display texture in the sense of internal structure and cohesion: there is the repetition of the words goat and lid, the anaphoric it, and the marked tonic on shouldn't showing that the following eat lid is to be interpreted as 'Given', as recoverable from what has gone before. In other words Nigel is beginning to build up the third component in the adult semantic system, the textual or text-forming component. In the adult language there are two parts to this: one based on structure, the other based on cohesion. The former consists of the theme and information systems of the clause, expressed through word order, nominalizations of various kinds, and the distribution into 'Given' and 'New' that is realized by intonation, by the placing of the tonic or primary stress. The latter consists of various anaphoric relations of reference, substitution, ellipsis, conjunction and collocation. Both these forms of texture begin to appear in Nigel's language quite early in Phase II.

Already in Phase I he has used intonation as a text-forming device, when he distinguishes between a͞ːːdà (mid falling) 'what's that?' and a̅:̅dà (high falling) 'and what's *that*?'. But the contrastive *location* of tonic prominence cannot arise until there is structure; and instances of it begin to appear around NL 7. Examples are:

N. put bemax down on **táble**   M. It is on the table.   N. **níla** table ('on *my* table!')

N. dada got scrambled **ègg** . . . mummy get **fóryou** scrambled egg ('get some for *me*!')

N. big **nòise**   M. What made a big noise?   N. **drìll** make big noise

About the same time, the first cohesive patterns begin to appear: first substitution (<u>one</u>), then reference (<u>it</u>, <u>that</u>), then conjunction (<u>but</u>). The reference items <u>it</u> and <u>that</u> occur first in what is generally assumed to be their primary meaning, that of reference to the situation: have it!, have that!, why broken that?; their use in text reference follows somewhat later. The substitute <u>one</u>, on the other hand, occurs from the start in contexts where it is both situationally and textually relevant—where the object is present *and* the word for which <u>one</u> is substituting has already been used, e.g. big one 'big bubble' while blowing bubbles and talking about them. Conjunction comes a little way behind, the first instance being in NL 9: that tree got no lèaf on . . . thát tree got leaf on but that tree got no lèaf on, which also has the marked tonic on that in the clause immediately preceding the <u>but</u>. As an instance of a number of these patterns coming together, the following is a typical specimen of dialogue from NL 9:

N. chuffa walk on ràilway line (2) . . . fast chùffa . . . one day might gò on fast chuffa (2)   F. Yes, we might.   N. one day go on blue chùffa . . . next chuffa còming . . . go on thàt one

5. THE IMAGINATIVE FUNCTION

This last is in an imaginary setting; the conversation actually takes place in the home. It illustrates the third semiotic mode, the imaginative, which is always present as a subsidiary theme in the development of meaning. Imaginative uses of language tend to have a phonology of their own; we saw in Phase I that the forms of verbal play tended to be distinct both in intonation and in other respects—naturally, since verbal play includes phonological play, with its rhyming and chiming and other types of sound pattern. (The most elaborated form of phonological play is of course singing, which is playing with the intonation and rhythm system.) But the system lends itself to play at all levels, and from this develops the semantic invention that emerges as a feature of Phase II—the use of the meaning potential to create a fictional environment. The recall function plays an essential part in this; when Nigel imagines to himself 'next chuffa coming . . . go on that one', he is also recalling past events in which this would have been appropriate discourse and may actually have been said. In the same way most of a young child's story-telling is a stringing together of recollections, either of past events or of stories told to him. Hence the vehicle for this kind of imaginative use of language is the mathetic mode, and the generic form is that of narrative. So clearly is this so that we tend to use the term 'narrative' in ordinary discourse to refer primarily to fictional narrative. But it is worth remembering that narrative develops first as a strategy for learning, and that it is only when the ideational potential comes to be combined with the imaginative function (which has developed independently of it) that fictional narrative is born.

Even when Nigel does begin to use meaning as a form of play, however, it is game-play that predominates rather than pretend-play. Indeed the earliest instance of semantic pretence seems to have been the result of a misunderstanding: Nigel said I go shòpping, which probably, in the current state of flux of his person system, meant '(I see) you're going shopping'. It was interpreted, however, as 'I'm (pretending I'm) going shopping', and the response was 'Are you? What are you going to buy?' Nigel thereupon joined in the act and said 'Eggs'. If Nigel's original utterance was pretend-play, it is unique and remains so for some time. Much more typical of the imaginative context is an exchange such as that exemplified from earlier in NL 9, beginning eat chùffa(p. 100), in which Nigel plays a long verbal game—it is a game at every level, phonological, lexicogrammatical and se-mantic—around the theme of can't eat chuffa, can't eat man, can't eat book. It is not long before this sort of thing will make him laugh; the ability to laugh at meanings (as distinct from laughing at things, like the hole in Daddy's toothbrush) seems to be a Phase III accomplishment, dependent on the fully fledged status of the semantic system, but the ability to play with meanings is a noticeable feature of the transition.

The following charts (pp. 116–9) present a summary of the deveolpment outlined in this section, arranged under the headings of pragmatic and mathetic. All the examples cited appear in the lists given in Section 5. It is hoped that this rather sketchy summary gives some idea of the progress of one child through the transitional stage linking his creation of a first 'infant' language with his mastery of the adult system. It should be emphasized once again that his entry into what we are calling Phase III, at about the end of his second year, does not mean that he has mastered the English language. It means that he has constructed for himself a three-level semiotic system which is organized the way the adult language is. It is English and not any other language, just as a tulip bud is a tulip and not a chrysanthemum or a rose. But it still has a long way to go before it comes into full flower.

PRAGMATIC

Goods   Things   Services   Persons (control)   Persons (interaction)

Eatables
rusk toast
biscuit cake
krispies egg
yellow
('syrup')
nuts

Playthings ⟨'not toys'⟩
keys beads
crown lipstick
book ball
dandelion

Ritual objects
powder
cottonwool
toothbrush
toothpaste

Music
Dvořák
Bartók ('Hey diddle') diddle
('Kalenda') Maia

Action ⟨'you . . . !'⟩
lick ('spoon')
('make') hole
('come for') lunch
('open') door
('lift me') up

Joint action ⟨'lets . . . !'⟩
('look at') book
('go for') walk
('draw') dog
dust

Permission ⟨'I want to . . .'⟩
('throw') stone
('call') Daddy
('get out &')
walk
('put') stick-
('in') hole
('go where I
was given')
chocolate

Excursion ⟨'let's go out & see . . .'⟩
car bus
train
stick hole
dog duck
weathercock

Greetings
hullo (+personal-ized)
Mummy
Daddy
Anna
cat
(seeking/finding)

Routines ⟨'I'm a . . .'⟩
puppy
devil

Sharings ⟨'look . . . !'⟩
'look what
I've done'
'look it's
broken!'
'what's that?'

+ search
where Dada
Mummy come

+ name play
Anna ! (—
Nigel !) —
Anna ! . . .

+locative
now ('let's go
to Daddy's')
room

Postural ⟨'sit') down
('I want to')
get-down

bounce (orange
on) table
hit (floor with)
hammer
⟨'I'm going to . . .'⟩

go Abbeywood
on train
⟨Excursion⟩

Mood : interrogative

+ Process
mend train
take it off

+ State
train stuck

play trains
play lions
⟨'let's . . .'⟩

+ Circumstance

take marmite
('into') kitchen

carry ('me')
high wall
(='catch me'
⟨'you . . . !'⟩

play highwall
('with me holding')
matchstick

train under tunnel;
get it for you

Dada put
all-together egg

make cross typewriter
in Dada room
Dada sing song
about duck

+ for
('draw') star
for-you
('for me')

find for-you
open for-you

+ Assistance
help ('me
with') juice

Anna help ('with')
greenpeas

butter on
Bartók on

+ supplementary
more egg
more toast
&c.

+ 'on'
butter on

+ 2nd element

+ Property
toothpaste on
red toothbrush

butter on
knife

In dialogue :
put Bemax on table. (—It
is on the table)—Nigel
table ('on my table !')

NL 6

NL 7

NL 8

116

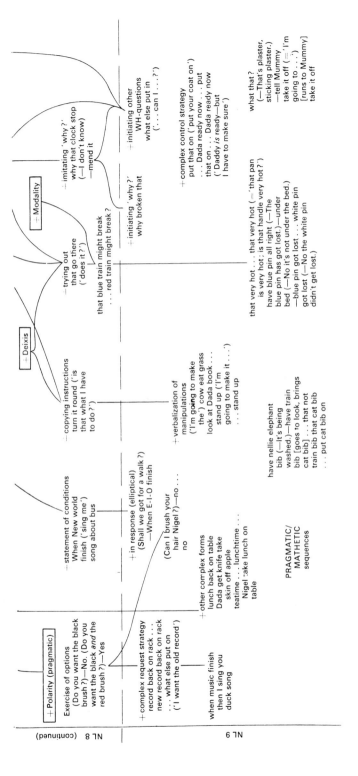

NL 8 (continued)

NL 9

+ Polarity (pragmatic)

Exercise of options
(Do you want the black brush?)—No. (Do you want the black *and* the red brush?)—Yes

+ complex request strategy
record back on rack . . .
new record back on rack
. . . what else put on
('I want the old record')

when music finish
then I sing you
duck song

— statement of conditions
When New world finish ('sing me') song about bus

+ in response (elliptical)
(Shall we got for a walk?)
—When E-I-O finish

(Can I brush your hair Nigel?)—no . . .
no

+ other complex forms
lunch back on table
Dada get knife take
skin off apple
teatime . . . lunchtime . . .
Nigel :ake lunch on
table

PRAGMATIC/
MATHETIC
sequences

+ Deixis

— copying instructions
turn it round ('is
that what I have
to do?')

+ verbalization of
manipulations
('I'm going to make
the') cow eat grass
look at Dada book . . .
stand up ('I'm
going to make it . . .')
. . . stand up

have nellie elephant
bib (—It's being
washed.)—have train
bib [goes to look, brings
cat bib] . . . that not
train bib that cat bib
. . . put cat bib on

— trying out
that go there
('does it?')

that blue train might break
. . . red train might break?

+ initiating 'why?'
why broken that

that very hot . . . that very hot (='that pan
is very hot; is that handle very hot?')
have blue pin all right (—The
blue pin has got lost.)—under
bed (—No it's not under the bed.)
—blue pin got lost . . . white pin
got lost (—No the white pin
didn't get lost.)

+ Modality

+ imitating 'why?'
why that clock stop
(—I don't know)
—mend it

+ initiating other
WH-questions
what else put in
('. . . can I . . . ?')

+ complex control strategy
put that on ('put your coat on')
. . . put
that on . . . Dada ready now . . . put
. . . Dada ready now . . . Dada ready
('Daddy *is* ready—but
I have to make sure')

what that?
(—That's plaster,
sticking plaster.)
—tell Mummy
take it off (='I'm
going to . . .')
[runs to Mummy]
take it off

117

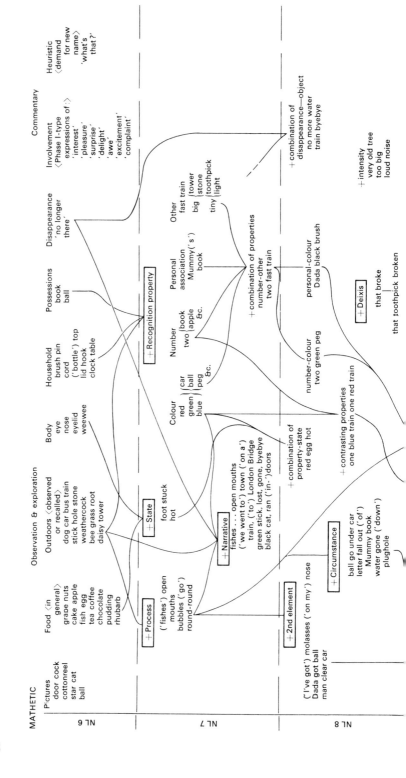

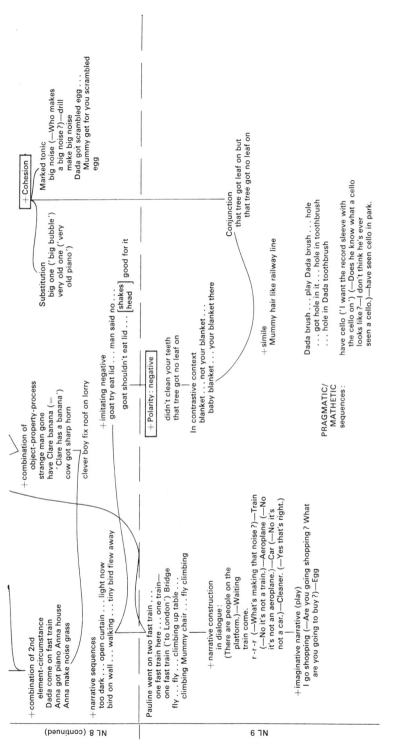

+ Cohesion

Substitution
big one ('big bubble')
very old one ('very
old piano')

Marked tonic
big noise (—Who makes
a big noise?)—drill
make big noise
Dada got scrambled egg...
Mummy get for you scrambled
egg

NL 8 (continued)

+combination of 2nd
element-circumstance
Dada come on fast train
Anna got piano Anna house
Anna make noise grass

+combination of
object-property-process
strange man gone
have Clare banana (=
'Clare has a banana')
cow got sharp horn

clever boy fix roof on lorry

+narrative sequences
too dark... open curtain... light now
bird on wall... walking... tiny bird flew away

+imitating negative
goat try eat lid... man said no...
goat shouldn't eat lid... [shakes head] good for it

+Polarity: negative

didn't clean your teeth
that tree got no leaf on

In contrastive context
blanket... not your blanket...
baby blanket... your blanket there

+simile
Mummy hair like railway line

Conjunction
that tree got leaf on but
that tree got no leaf on

NL 9

Pauline went on two fast train...
one fast train here... one train—
one fast train ('to London') Bridge
fly... fly... climbing up table...
climbing Mummy chair... fly climbing

+narrative construction
in dialogue:
(There are people on the
platform.)—Waiting
train come.
r-r-r (—What's making that noise?)—Train
(—No it's not a train.)—Aeroplane (—No
it's not an aeroplane.)—Car (—No it's
not a car.)—Cleaner. (—Yes that's right.)

+imaginative narrative (play)
I go shopping (—Are you going shopping? What
are you going to buy?)—Egg

PRAGMATIC/
MATHETIC
sequences:

Dada brush... play Dada brush... hole
... got hole in it... hole in toothbrush
... hole in Dada toothbrush

have cello ('I want the record sleeve with
the cello on') (—Does he know what a cello
looks like?—I don't think he's ever
seen a cello.)—have seen cello in park.

119

6 The social context of language development

1. Learning the language and learning the culture

In the previous discussion we have been concentrating on the issue of how a child learns language. How does he construct a meaning potential, a semantic system together with its patterns of realization in lexicogrammar and in phonology? In the present chapter we shall focus attention on a question which is rather different from this one, the question of how a child learns the culture. How does he construct a social system, an interpretative model of the environment in which he finds himself? In other words, how does he construct reality?

It is a commonplace that the child's construction of reality is achieved largely through the medium of language. But to say this does not resolve the puzzle; if anything, it enhances it. It is not as if anyone teaches a child the mysteries of the social system— the social structure, systems of knowledge, systems of values and the like. Yet before he ever comes to school he has accumulated a vast store of information about these things; and he has done so not only without instruction but without those from whom he has learnt it being aware that they know it themselves. And he has learnt it largely through language: through the small change of everyday speech, the casual linguistic interaction of the home, the street and the neighbourhood.

The learning of language and the learning of culture are obviously two different things. At the same time, they are closely interdependent. This is true not only in the sense that a child constructs a reality for himself largely through language, but also in the more fundamental sense that language is itself a part of this reality. The linguistic system is a part of the social system. Neither can be learnt without the other.

In the fourth chapter we suggested a way of conceptualizing the social system and the linguistic system that would enable the two to be brought into some sort of relevant relationship with one another in a developmental context. We took the view of the social system as a semiotic, a system of meanings that is *realized through* (inter alia) the linguistic system. The linguistic semiotic—that is, semantics—is one form of the realization of the social semiotic. There are many other symbolic systems through which the meanings of the culture are expressed: art forms, social structures and social institutions, educational and legal systems, and the like. But in the developmental process language is the primary one. A child's construction of a semantic system and his construction of a social system take place side by side, as two aspects of a single unitary process.

In the process of building up the social semiotic, the network of meanings that constitutes the culture, the child is becoming a member of the species 'social man'. This carries all the same implications as are present in our characterization of the social system as a semiotic. Social man is, effectively, 'sociosemiotic man', man as a repository of social meanings. The child builds up a potential for exchanging the meanings that are engendered by the system (and, so, in the long run, for modifying the system—since the social system is a system of meanings, it is constituted out of innumerable acts of meaning which shape and determine the system). We can watch this process taking place at all stages in the child's development of a language.

Consider the following examples, all taken from Nigel at 2;11 (two years eleven months) in verbal exchanges with his mother:

(1) MOTHER [having fetched Nigel home from school]: How on earth did you get all that sand in your hair? NIGEL: I was just standing up and I threw the sand to it [='at it'; referent unspecified] and it got in my hair. MOTHER: And what did the teacher say? NIGEL: No . . . because it was time to go home and have your [='my'] pieces of meat.

(2) NIGEL [from playroom]: Mummy where are the ones with green in? MOTHER: The what? NIGEL: The all green ones. MOTHER: But I don't know what it is you're talking about. NIGEL [patiently]: The ones I had in Nairobi. [Mother gives up.]

(3) NIGEL [at teatime]: What day is it today? MOTHER: It's Thursday. NIGEL: There's no school on Thursday. MOTHER: There is—you've already been to school. NIGEL: I mean . . . what comes after Thursday? MOTHER: Friday. There's school on Friday too. NIGEL: But you can't [='I can't'] go to school on Friday yet. MOTHER: No, it hasn't started being Friday yet.

Specimens such as these, at a first glance, show the gulf between the child's world of meaning and that of the adult. Nigel's concept of the relations between events is not that of the adult. The sand got in his hair because that's the way things happen, not as you plan them; and he was told not to throw sand because it was time for lunch ('time to go home and have your pieces of meat'). His working out of divisions of time is far from complete: he knows that days succeed one another and have different names, but is not very clear just when the changeover takes place ('But you can't go to school on Friday yet'—i.e. Friday, on which I go to school next, hasn't started yet?). He cannot conceive that the person he is talking to is unable to identify an object that is in his own focus of attention ('Mummy where are the ones with green in?', with no clue given as to what is presupposed by the substitute ones; cf. it in 'threw the sand to it'). At the same time, on closer inspection, the examples show how the linguistic interaction in which the child takes part, while it reveals semiotic incompatibilities of all kinds, also provides him with the means of learning the semiotic of the adult culture. It is very clear to Nigel that his own meanings fail to get across in example 2; and he is himself clearly searching for meanings in 3. Even in example 1 the cultural concept of rational action is present, and is in fact foregrounded by Nigel himself, although his own attempts at applying it are not quite what the adult semiotic prescribes.

We can see all the time, if we pay attention to what is said by, to and in the presence of a small child, how in the course of the most ordinary linguistic interaction he is constantly learning the structure of the environment in which he is growing up, in all its aspects, material, logical, institutional and social. He is also, at the same time, developing his own unique personality, which is being formed at the intersection of a whole number of role relationships which are themselves likewise part of the semiotic structure of his universe. It is one thing, of course, to recognize that all this is taking place, and that it is taking place through the medium of language. It is quite another thing to explain how it happens, and how the linguistic system is endowed with the potential for making it happen.

In principle, a child is learning one semiotic system, the culture, and simultaneously he is learning the means of learning it—a second semiotic system, the language, which is the intermediary in which the first one is encoded. This is a very complex situation. In order to sort it out, let us first identify the various components which make up the total picture of language as social interaction, as expression of the social semiotic. Having considered each of these separate components in turn, we shall then try to integrate them into some sort of a composite pattern.

2. Text and meaning

Let us first consider the language people produce and react to, what they say and write, and read and listen to, in the course of daily life. This we shall refer to as *text*. Any instance of language that is operational, as distinct from citational (like sentences in a grammar book, or words listed in a dictionary), is text. The term covers both speech and writing, and is quite neutral as regards style and content: it may be language in action, conversation, telephone talk, debate, dramatic dialogue, narrative fiction, poetry, prayer, inscriptions, public notices, legal proceedings, communing with animals, intimate monologue or anything else.

From birth onwards, a child is surrounded by text. There is a constant exchange of meanings going on all around him, in which he is in one way or another involved. It should not be forgotten, in this regard, that he listens to a vast quantity of text in the form of dialogue in which he is not himself a participant. It was at 3 ; 1 (three years one month) that Nigel began formulating to himself the difference between being a participant in an exchange and being an onlooker; he used to ask, very frequently over just a few weeks until he was satisfied he understood the principle, 'Were you saying that to me?' Where the child is a participant he is, of course, a co-author of the text.

What are the essential properties of text? It is meaning, and it is choice. In the first place, text is meaning. We think of text first of all as words and sentences; and it is, certainly, encoded in words and sentences—in just the same way as those words and sentences are further encoded in sounds, or in letters. But text is not made of sounds or letters; and in the same way it is not made of words and phrases and clauses and sentences. It is made of meanings, and encoded in wordings, soundings and spellings. In other words, we are locating text at the semantic level. A text is a semantic unit, realized as (encoded in) lexicogrammatical units which are further realized as (recoded in) phonological or orthographic units.

Secondly, text is choice. A text represents a selection within numerous sets of options; everything that is said presupposes a

123

background of what might have been said but was not. In linguistic terms, each decision of the speaker—each microlinguistic act, as it were—presupposes a paradigmatic environment, a set of options that have the potentiality of being selected under the given conditions. This is the background of what might have been. Since we have defined the text in semantic terms, however, we should replace *say* by *mean*. Text is 'what is meant'—presupposing a background of what might have been meant but was not. The microlinguistic acts, or countless small choices that the speaker makes as he goes along, are actually microsemantic acts; what the speaker is doing is meaning. Hence a text is a semantic structure that is formed out of a continuous process of choice among innumerable interrelated sets of semantic options.

We are referring to the total set of such semantic options as the 'meaning potential'. The meaning potential is what can be meant —the potential of the semantic system. This is what we have been following through in its earliest phases in Chapters 2–5, asking how Nigel started building up a meaning potential and what it looked like at different stages in its construction, in the course of its development. Text represents the actualization of this meaning potential. So everything the child says is interpreted—not just by a linguist, but by those who interact with the child in daily life— as a pattern of selection within the meanings that make up his semantic system at that time. This is what we mean by referring to text as semantic choice; and it explains why the mother understands everything the child says, much of which unintelligible to those outside the circuit of his daily life. They do not know the child's meaning potential.

There are two ways of looking at the meaning potential. We may interpret it in the context of the situation, or we may interpret it in the context of the culture (still using Malinowski's all-important distinction). We may choose to think of the meaning potential as being the whole semantic system of the language; or we may choose to think of it in the form of specific sub-systems each of which (or each set of which) is associated with a particular class of situations. The former is a fiction; we cannot describe the whole semantic system. The latter is also, of course, a fiction; but it may be a more accessible one. It may be possible to represent the meaning potential in the form of sets of options that are specific to a given situation type.

This is in fact what we have been doing from the start. The headings 'instrumental', 'regulatory' and so on are the headings, the points of entry, of semantic systems that are associated with specific social contexts. A child constructs his meaning potential just in this way, by building up context-specific micro-paradigms, small sets of options that are his resource for each of the types of situation that serve, for him, as environments of symbolic action. At first, as we have pointed out, these are insulated one from another; the system allows just one meaning at a time. But later they come to be combined; and, as we saw, it is the combination of meanings from different functions that leads to the re-interpretation of the notion of 'function' itself, first as a generalized context of use (the 'macro-functions' of pragmatic and mathetic) and subsequently as an abstract component of the system (the 'meta-functions' of ideational and interpersonal).

3. Other components of the social semiotic

Meanwhile the meanings by which the child is surrounded are, as always, meanings in context. They relate to their environment, and are interpreted in relation to their environment—to the context of situation, in other words. The *situation* is the medium in which text lives and breathes. This, as we have seen, is the Malinowskian concept of 'context of situation' as made explicit and modified by Firth, who pointed out that it had to be seen not as an aggregate of concrete spatio-temporal goings-on, a sort of ornamental backdrop of sights and sounds, but as an abstract representation of the relevant environment of the text. In modern jargon, it is the ecology of the text. It is a characteristic of the adult language system that the text it engenders is not tied to the immediate scenario as its relevant environment. The context of situation of a text may be entirely remote from what is happening around the act of speaking or writing.

Consider a traditional story as it is told by a mother to her child at bedtime. Here the context of situation is on two levels. On the one hand there is the immediate environment, the interaction of mother and child under particular circumstances that are associated with intimacy and relaxation. On the other hand there is the fictive environment conjured by the text itself, the imaginary world of wolves and woodcutters in which the events described take place. It is only in very strictly pragmatic contexts, those of language in action as it has been called, where the text is simply an ancillary to some activity that the participants are engaged in, that the context of situation can be identified with the visible and tangible phenomena surrounding the text: and even here, these phenomena are likely to be endowed with social values.

For this reason we are interpreting the concept of 'situation' in still more abstract terms, as a semiotic structure deriving from the totality of meaning relations that constitutes the social system. This makes it possible to talk not so much about the particulars of this or that actual context of situation in which a given text is located but rather about the set of general features that characterizes a certain *situation type*. The way in which a generalized context of situation, or situation type, might be represented as a semiotic construct will be discussed in the next section.

The first two of the concepts to be brought into relation, therefore, are those of text and situation: text as semantic choice, and situation as the semiotic environment of text. The third to be added to these is the concept of *register*. The register is the semantic variety of which a text is an instance.

A register can be defined as a particular configuration of meanings that is associated with a particular situation type. In any social context, certain semantic resources are characteristically employed; certain sets of options are as it were 'at risk' in the given semiotic environment. These define the register. Considered in terms of the notion of meaning potential, the register is the range of meaning potential that is activated by the semiotic properties of the situation.

To return to the same example, there are certain types of meanings that are typically associated with traditional stories as told to children. These are not simply thing-meanings, names of persons and animals and objects and events that typically figure in such stories, though these are a part of the picture; but also characteristic role relationships, chains of events, patterns of dialogue, and special types of complex semantic structures such as are represented in expressions like <u>and she was so (frightened, &c.) that she (ran and ran,</u> &c.); <u>but the third time he tried, he (managed to reach,</u> &c.). The set of such typical meanings and combinations of meanings constitutes the register of traditional children's narratives in very many cultures and sub-cultures.

The fourth major component of the sociolinguistic universe is the *linguistic system* itself. The difficulty with notions like text and situation lies not so much in their own definition and interpretation as in the relating of them to the linguistic system as a whole. In what way does a particular text draw on the resources of the linguistic system? How can we see the meanings that the child encodes on any particular occasion in relation to the potential that lies behind them? This is a perspective that it is easy to lose sight of if one is focussing attention on the text, on what a child has actually said or had said to him. But it is of great importance in our understanding of the developmental picture. We are interested in the potential of the system, and in how the child constructs the system. This means not merely being able to analyze a particular piece of text so as to reveal what are the structures underlying it, but also being able to show what are the options that are expressed by those structures and what is the total set of options that the child has at his disposal in that part of his semantic system. So for example we might recognize from something the child says that he can form a structure made up of the elements Actor + Process + Goal, as in Nigel's <u>man clean car</u> at 1 ; 8 (20 months). But we want to know what semantic option this represents, in the sense of what is the type of process that he encodes in this way; and what other types of process does he recognize—in other words, what is the semantic system that he has at this stage for the representation of the processes of action, thought, feeling and so on that come within the realm of his experience? The concept of register becomes especially important here, as the system expands, because it forms a bridge between the system and the text.

In the present context, what concerns us most within the linguistic system is the semantic system. We are considering the semantic system not from a conceptual but from a functional point of view, as a potential in respect of certain semiotic operations; and in particular we are considering its organization into basic components which are of a functional kind. In the language of a small child, these components are specific to the social context, or situation type: they are the instrumental, regulatory and other components of the Phase I system. In the adult language, however, the functional components of the semantics are no longer specific to the context; they are general to all contexts. Whatever the particular situation type, the meanings that are expressed are of three kinds, which we have called 'ideational', 'interpersonal' and 'textual'.

The infinitely varied properties of different situations, the types of activity, the role relationships, and the symbolic channels, are all realized through selections in these three areas of meaning potential. The ideational represents the potential of the system for the speaker as an observer: it is the content function of language, language as about something. The interpersonal is the potential of the system for the speaker as an intruder: it is the participatory function of language, language as doing something. The textual is the potential of the system for the creation of text: it is the relevance function of language, whereby the meanings derived from the other functional components relate to the environment and thus become operational.

These are the functional components of the adult semantic system; with only trivial exceptions (such as Hi! as a greeting, which presumably has no ideational element in its makeup), any adult exchange of meanings involves all three components. Whatever the particular use of language on this or that occasion, whatever the subject-matter and the genre and the purpose of the communication, there will be a choice of content, a choice of interaction type, and a choice of texture. These are the different kinds of meaning potential of the system. But they are also the formally definable components of the lexicogrammatical system; these different semantic realms appear as clearly defined, mutually independent sets of options at the formal level. It is this that enables, and disposes, the child to learn the lexicogrammar: since the system is organized along functional lines, it relates closely to what the child can see language doing as he observes it going on around him.

The fifth and final element in the sociolinguistic universe is the *social structure*. This term is being used in a way which is not synonymous with 'social system'. The social system is the broader term; it encompasses all the elements that make up the picture, and much else besides—it is more or less equivalent to 'the culture'. The social structure refers specifically to the organization of society. This permeates all forms of interaction and exchange of meanings by the members; but it enters into the picture that we are building up here in two significant ways. In the first place it is a part of the environment; hence it is a part of what is being transmitted to the child through language. In the second place it is a determinant of the transmission process, since it determines the types of role relationship in the 'primary socializing agencies', the social groups through which a child takes out his membership of the culture—the family, the young children's peer group, and the school—and so creates the conditions in which the child lives and learns. Our understanding of how this happens is very largely due to Bernstein. Bernstein's work demonstrates that the social structure is not just a kind of incidental appendage to linguistic interaction, as linguists have tended to think of it, but is an integral element in the deeper processes that such interaction involves.

If a child learns the culture from ordinary everyday linguistic interaction, as he certainly does, we must suppose not only that he decodes what he hears correctly in a way that is specifically relevant to the context of situation but also that he interprets it correctly in a way that is generally relevant to the context of culture. In other words if his mother tells him off he not only knows that he is being told off but also learns something in the process about the value systems of the culture he is participating in. This pre-supposes that the linguistic system must be coherent not only within itself but also with the culture; not only are the semantic options which make up the meaning potential *realized* explicitly in the lexicogrammar—they are also themselves *realizing* the higher-order meanings of the social semiotic. All the elements mentioned above play some part in the total picture.

4. Structure of the social context

From a sociological point of view a text is meaningful not so much because we do not know what the speaker is going to say, as in a mathematical model of communication, as because we do know. Given certain facts, we can predict a good deal of what is coming with a significantly high probability of being right. This is not, of course, to deny the creative aspect of language and of text. The speaker can always prove us wrong; and in any case, his behaviour is none the less creative even if our predictions are fulfilled to the letter.

What are these 'certain facts'? They are the general properties of the situation, in the abstract sense in which the term is being used here. Essentially what we need to know is the semiotic structure of the situation.

A number of linguists, notably Firth, Pike and Hymes, have suggested interesting ways of characterizing the context of situation. Hymes' list of categories could be summarized as follows: form and content of the message, setting, participants, ends (intent and effect), key, medium, genre and interactional norms. The problem is, however, to know what kind of status and validity to accord to a conceptual framework such as this one. Are these to be thought of as descriptive categories providing a framework for the interpretation of text in particular situation instances, as conceived of by Malinowski? Or are they predictive concepts providing a means for the determination of text in generalized situation types?

Either of these would be of interest; but in the present context, in which we are trying to see how a child constructs the social system out of text instances, and are therefore concerned to relate text, situation and linguistic system, it is the second of these perspectives which we need to adopt. We are thinking not in terms of this or that situation but of a situation type, a generalized social context in which text is created; and of the situational factors not merely as descriptive but as constitutive of the text. The semiotic properties of the situation specify the register, the semantic configurations that characterize text associated with that type of situation—the meaning potential that the speaker will typically draw on.

So if we set up a conceptual framework for the representation of situation types, we do so in order that the categories we use will serve to predict features of the text. But this is not enough. Such categories are two-faced; they not only related 'downwards' to the text but also 'upwards' to some higher order of abstraction—in this case, two such higher orders, the social and the linguistic. In other words the concepts that we use in describing a 'situation type', or social context, whatever concepts they are, have to be interpretable both in terms of the culture and in terms of the linguistic system.

The second of these requirements is particularly strong, since it is not immediately obvious how situational factors like the setting, the statuses and roles of the participants, and the like, can relate to linguistic categories. But it is this requirement which may lead us to select one from among the number of existing and possible schemes; and we shall return to one proposed some years ago by Halliday, McIntosh & Strevens, which was a three-fold analysis in terms of the concepts of *field*, *tenor* and *mode*. It was not entirely clear at the time why such a scheme should be preferred, except that intuitively it seemed simpler than most others. But it can now be seen to offer a means of making an essential link between the linguistic system and the text.

A framework of this general kind has been discussed subsequently by a number of writers on the subject, for example Spencer & Gregory in *Linguistics and Style*, Doughty, Pearce & Thornton in *Exploring Language*, Halliday in *Language and Social Man*, and Ure & Ellis in 'Register in descriptive linguistics and descriptive sociology'. We can relate the general concepts of field, tenor and mode to the categories set out by Hymes in 'Models of interaction of language and social setting' as these were summarized above. A situation type, or social context, as we understand it, is characterized by a particular semiotic structure, a complex of features which sets it apart from other situation types. This structure can then be interpreted on three dimensions: in terms of the ongoing activity (field), the role relationships involved (tenor), and the symbolic or rhetorical channel (mode). The first of these, the field, corresponds roughly to Hymes' 'setting' and 'ends'; it is the field of action, including symbolic action, in which the text has its meaning. It therefore includes what we usually call 'subject-matter', which is not an independent feature but is a function of the type of activity. The second, the tenor, which corresponds in general terms to Hymes' 'participants' and 'key', refers to the role relationships that are embodied in the situation, which determine levels of formality and speech styles but also very much alse besides. The third heading, that of mode, is roughly Hymes' 'instrumentalities' and 'genre'; this refers to the symbolic channel or wavelength selected, which is really the semiotic function or functions assigned to language in the situation. Hence this includes the distinction between speech and writing as a special case.

Field, tenor and mode are not kinds of language use; still less are they varieties of language. Nor are they, however, simply generalized components of the speech situation. They are, rather, the environmental determinants of text. Given an adequate specification of the situation in terms of field, tenor and mode, we ought to be able to make certain predictions about the linguistic properties of the text that is associated with it: that is, about the register, the configurations of semantic options that typically feature in this environment, and hence also about the grammar and vocabulary, which are the realizations of the semantic options. The participants in the situation themselves make just such predictions. It is one of the features of the social system, as a semiotic system, that the members can and do make significant predictions about the meanings that are being exchanged, predictions which depend on their interpretation of the semiotics of the situation type in which they find themselves. This is an important aspect of the potential of the system, and it is this that we are trying to characterize.

The possibility of making such predictions appears to arise because the categories of field, tenor and mode, which we are using to describe the semiotics of the situation, are in their turn associated in a systematic way with the functional components of the semantic system. This is not, of course, a coincidence. The semantic system evolved, we assume, operationally, as a form of symbolic interaction in social contexts; so there is every reason that it should reflect the structure of such contexts in its own internal organization.

We referred above to the tripartite functional composition of the adult semantic system, with its components of ideational, interpersonal and textual. It was mentioned that this scheme was not something that is arrived at from the outside; this organization is clearly present in the lexicogrammatical system—as seen, for example, in the threefold structuring of the clause in English in terms of transitivity (ideational), mood (interpersonal) and theme (textual). Now it appears that each of these different components of meaning is typically activated by a corresponding component in the semiotic structure of the situation. Thus, the *field* is associated with the *ideational* component, the *tenor* with the *interpersonal* component, and the *mode* with the *textual* component.

Let us see how this works, using another example from Nigel's interaction with his mother, this time at age 1 ; 11 (23 months).

Text. Nigel at age 1; 11.

MOTHER [in bathroom, Nigel sitting on chair]: Now you wait there till I get your facecloth. Keep sitting there. [But Nigel is already standing up on the chair.] NIGEL [in exact imitation of mother's intonation pattern, not in a correcting intonation]: Keep standing thére. Put the mug on the flóor. MOTHER: Put the mug on the floor? What do you want? NIGEL: Daddy tòothbrush. MOTHER: Oh you want Daddy's toothbrush do you? NIGEL: Yés . . . you (='I') want to put the fròg in the múg. MOTHER: I think the frog is too big for the mug. NIGEL: Yes you can put the dùck in the múg . . . make búbble . . . make búbble. MOTHER: Tomorrow. Nearly all the water's run out. NIGEL: You want Mummy red tóothbrush . . . yes you can have Mummy old red tóothbrush.

Situational features.

Field: Personal toilet, assisted (mother washing child) ; concurrently (child) exploring (i) container principle (i.e. putting things in things) and (ii) ownership and acquisition of property (i.e. getting things that belong to other people).

Tenor: Mother and small child interaction; mother determining course of action; child pursuing own interests, seeking permission; mother granting permission and sharing child's interests, but keeping her own course in view.

Mode: Spoken dialogue; pragmatic speech ('language-in-action'), the mother's guiding, the child's furthering (accompanying or immediately preceding) the actions to which it is appropriate; co-operative, without conflict of goals.

Determination of linguistic features by situational features.

Field determines: transitivity patterns—the types of process, e.g. relational clauses, possessive (get, have) and circumstantial: locative (put); material process clauses, spatial: posture (sit, stand); also the minor processes, e.g. circumstantial: locative (in); perhaps the tenses (simple present); and the *content* aspect of the vocabulary, e.g. naming of objects.
All these belong to the *ideational* component of the semantic system.
Tenor determines: patterns of mood, e.g. [mother] imperative (you wait, keep sitting) and of modality, e.g. [child] permission (want to, can, and non-finite forms such as make bubble meaning 'I want to be allowed to . . .'); also of person, e.g. [mother] "second person" (you), [child] "first person" (you = 'I'). and of key, represented by the system of intonation (pitch contour, e.g. child's systematic opposition of rising tone, demanding a response, versus falling tone, not demanding a response).
All these belong to the *interpersonal* component of the semantic system.
Mode determines: forms of cohesion, e.g. question-&-answer with the associated type of ellipsis (What do you want?—Daddy toothbrush); the patterns of voice and theme, e.g. active voice with child as subject/theme; the forms of deixis, e.g. exophoric (situation-referring) the (the mug, &c); and the lexical continuity, e.g. repetition of mug, toothbrush, put in.
All these belong to the *textual* component of the semantic system.

5. Semiotic strategies

What this example suggests is that there is a general tendency whereby different elements in the context of situation call for different components of the semantics—different aspects of the meaner's ability to mean. The situation is a semiotic structure, consisting essentially of a doing part and a being part: a social process (things going on), and associated role relationships and role interaction (persons taking part). The nature of the social process tends to be expressed through ideational meanings, and the nature of the role relationships through interpersonal meanings. Meanings of the third kind, the textual, express the particular semiotic

133

mode that is being adopted. The meanings are expressed, in their turn, through the medium of the lexicogrammatical system; and hence there is a systematic, though indirect, link between grammatical structure and the social context. This is the central feature of the environment in which a child learns language. Since everything that he hears is text—language that is operational in a context of situation—the fact that it is systematically related to this context is the guarantee of its significance for the learning process. It is this that makes language learnable.

We shall return to this point briefly in a final discussion below. Meanwhile we should remember that from the child's point of view learning how to mean is like learning any other form of activity. It is something he has to master, and it has to be broken down into manageable tasks. This breaking down process is at once both cognitive and social. We know from the work of Piaget and Sinclair de Zwart that the meaning potential is cognitively ordered; certain meanings will be learnt before others, and this is an aspect of the biological processes of maturation. But there is an environmental aspect to this too. The functional system with which the child is operating at any given moment acts as a filter on the semantic input, so that he processes just those elements which are consonant, or resonant, with his semiotic potential at that time.

It is not easy to illustrate this except by inspection of large quantities of data, in which whatever is said to and around the child has been incorporated, together with relevant situational information. But the following short illustration will perhaps suggest what is meant. Nigel at 21 months (NL 8) had been for a walk with his father in Greenwich Park; they had paused, as often, to look at the Meridian Clock mounted in the Observatory wall. Unprecedentedly, it had stopped.

F. I wonder why that clòck's stopped? I've never known it stopped befŏre. Perhaps they're clèaning it, or mènding it.

They return home. Some hours later, on the same day, Nigel returns to the subject:

N. why that clóck stop
F. I don't know. Why do you think?
N. ménd it

Nigel's utterances are both on the rising, pragmatic tone. Now, many features of the text-in-situation constituted by the father's first remark are relevant as potential input: the mood of I wonder, the modality of perhaps, the temporal relation before, the collocation clean + clock, and so on. Looking at Nigel's later utterance, we see what he has in fact processed in the intervening period. The mood of I wonder has been translated into the pragmatic, response-demanding mode (note that none of the father's utterances was on a rising tone);—resulting in what is in fact the first WH-question recorded in Nigel's speech. The meaning 'response demanded' carries the potential of being extended to include 'verbal response demanded', the process being perhaps furthered by the open-ended modality of perhaps meaning 'supply "yes" or "no"'. He cannot of course answer a why question; but he retains the why from his father's utterance because it does chime in with a recognizable semiotic function. In mend it, mending has been reinterpreted in terms of this pragmatic function, which is the only context Nigel knows for 'mend' ('I want this to be mended'): cleaning has however been filtered out as irrelevant, presumably because although it is a word he knows— he had said man clean car some days previously—it has occurred only in mathetic contexts and is therefore functionally incompatible with mending. The result is an utterance which in terms of his pre-existing system would be interpreted as 'I want the clock to be mended', but which has the potentiality also for meaning 'will they mend it?' and even 'are they mending it?' The point is not that we are called on to decide which of these it actually meant; that question is undecidable, because those are not alternative meanings in Nigel's system. The point is that this little interchange plays its part in providing the conditions for the emergence of new meanings, in this case the yes/no question as a possible form of response-seeking semiotic act.

Such delayed reactions are often very suggestive indicators of the selective processing of meanings into the system. There is a clear functional limitation on the input; though rather than seeing it as a limitation we should see it as an interpretative device, a means of assimilating what comes in to what is already there in a way which also allows it to change what is already there. The functional organization of the existing meaning potential acts as a kind of semantic resonator capturing just those components of the input which are near enough to its own frequencies to be able to modify and expand it further.

For the child the overall context is one of survival, and he develops semiotic strategies such that he can use his meaning potential as he is building it and build it as he is using it. These are highly-valued patterns of meaning that play a significant part in the developmental process. They can be found at all levels in the system. A number of Nigel's general patterns already referred to could be included in this category; here is a summary of some of the more important ones in Phases I and II:

I. PHONOLOGICAL. The most obvious strategy here is the opposition of falling and rising tone, the realization of the mathetic/pragmatic opposition (which is itself the key semantic strategy for Phase II). The fall/rise opposition is the heart of the adult intonation system; all the complex tones, and all the meanings of the tones, can be explained on the basis of this simple system, in which falling means 'decided' (certain, complete &c.) and rising means 'undecided'. Nigel's Phase II system is not that of the adult language, naturally, since he has not learnt the various grammatical systems which determine its specific significance (for example, he has no mood system, and so cannot use falling/rising as the realization of sub-categories of indicative (declarative and interrogative) and imperative the way the adult does). But Nigel's use does reflect the basic meaning that the opposition between falling and rising has in English: falling means complete (no response demanded) and rising means incomplete—moreover rising, as in the adult language, is the marked term.

II. GRAMMATICAL. The fundamental grammatical strategy is structure, the combining of variables. At the beginning of Phase II, Nigel learns that new meaning results from the combination of elements one with another. He also learns that such combinations take two forms. (i) Univariate structures: combinations of variables each having the same value in the resulting configuration. The adult language has a number of such types of combination (for example co-ordination, apposition, subclassification); Nigel's only one at this stage is co-ordination, as in 'cars, buses, trains, stones, sticks and holes'. It is noticeable that for a time there is a minor but distinct phonological strategy associated with these: each element in a co-ordination must have two syllables (so bus, ordinarily ba, becomes baba; dog, ordinarily bɒuwɒu, does not change). (ii) Multivariate structures: combinations of elements having different values in the resulting configuration. Examples in early Phase II are: Supplementation + Desired object (more meat), Property + Class of object (green car), Process + Medium of process (open mouth). These are the prototypes of the multivariate structures that make up the nominal group and the clause of the adult language.

III. SEMANTIC. Phase II semantic strategies are the specific functional meanings of the mathetic and pragmatic modes. An example is the pragmatic strategies deriving from the Phase I regulatory function: requests for permission, requests for action, suggestions for joint action ('can I?', 'will you?', 'shall we?'). But in fact the entire functional interpretation that we are putting on the picture of Nigel's language development is nothing other than an interpretation of the semantic strategies that appear to be critical for his success in learning how to mean.

IV. SEMIOTIC. All those listed above are, in fact, semiotic strategies, since the term encompasses all aspects of the organization of meaning. But there are more general strategies which are strategies for the use of the linguistic system, ways of deploying the meaning potential, so to speak—sometimes with alternative, or accompanying, non-linguistic modes of realization. The child's aim is to be good at meaning, and from the start he locates himself in symbolic contexts in which semiotic success is significantly at risk. He undertakes meaning tasks which may fail, but which typically are rewarded if successful. Here are some examples:

(i) Reparatory strategies: what to do when meaning breaks down. The fundamental semiotic strategy of repeating loudly and slowly when not understood, which involves recognizing that meaning has not been successful, that this may result from a failure in the expression, and that the expression can be foregrounded as a way of overcoming the failure, develops remarkably early. A clear example is found in the material in the preceding chapter, section 5.1, from the beginning of NL 7 when Nigel has just reached 18 months. In the context of a list of things seen on a walk, Nigel says douba, which usually means 'toast'; his father tries that interpretation, but Nigel rejects it, repeating the word very slowly and distinctly. It happens that his father never does get the meaning on this occasion, and now never will; but the principle is established and Nigel does not abandon it.

(ii) Interaction strategies: semiotic interaction with others through shared attention to objects. This strategy appears at the very outset of the system, in NL 1; but it is a major motif in the evolution of the Phase II mathetic function. It has been discussed in the earlier chapters and need not be repeated here.

(iii) Development of instrumental forms. The semiotics of getting

what one wants goes through a number of strategic moments: Phase I nànànànà 'I want that'; Phase II, specific, e.g. more méat; general, háve it, háve that; Phase III, introduction of a mood system as in you want your meat 'I want my meat'. Those of Phases II and III may be accompanied by politeness forms, e.g. Phase II plɪmeyaya 'please may I have?', which make their function explicit.

(iv) Development of simile and metaphor. A fundamental semiotic strategy is the use of likeness as a mode of meaning, likeness between things that are essentially different. Recognizing a picture—identifying it as a representation—exemplifies the receptive form of this strategy. In its productive form it appears from NL 7 onwards; examples are 'Uncle's pipe blows smoke like a train' (cited in chapter 3; note that this itself depends on the symbolic representation of a train, since Nigel has never seen a steam train except in pictures) and Mummy hair like railway line (NL 9; see Chapter 5 section 5). Such metaphorical meanings characteristically relate to highly coded realms of experience—in Nigel's case, trains.

The interest of these and other semiotic strategies lies not only in the contribution they make to the learning of the language and the culture but also in the way in which they anticipate the adult communicative style. An adult, in his various registers, the semantic configurations that he typically associates with a given social context, tends especially in those well-tried social contexts that make up much of his daily semiotic activity to adopt various more or less routinized semiotic strategies, some of them being simply rules for the particular type of discourse and others more individual paths through the network of sociosemiotic interaction. In their extreme form, these are the 'games people play', mechanisms for mediating between the individual and social reality. But all exchange of meanings involves semiotic strategies. Thanks to the work of Sacks and Schegloff, we are gaining significant insights into the nature of these and their place in the social process. It is interesting to see them evolving in the developmental context, and an important question for current investigation is how far and in what specific ways they are a necessary component of learning.

6. Language development as an interactive process

We referred in Chapter 1 to the different emphases and contrasts in perspective that characterized the renewed interest in language development studies from the mid 1960's onwards, in particular the rather artificial polarization between two conceptions of language and language learning, one as genetically endowed and readymade, the other as environmentally fashioned and evolving. It is refreshing to find language development studies in the 1970's moving away from this rather sterile debate, in a direction which puts language in a less insulated and more relevant perspective. Language is no longer being thought of as an autonomous object; nor is language development seen any longer as a kind of spontaneous once-for-all happening resting on a given biological foundation, to be achieved by a certain maturational stage or not at all. This is not to deny, of course, the fact that there is a biological foundation to language; but simply to assert that language development is an aspect and a concomitant of ongoing developmental processes of a more general kind. As Lois Bloom put it, "The beginning of the 1970's marked a major shift in research in language development, away from the description of child language in terms of linguistic theory and towards the explanation of language development in terms of cognitive theory"; and her own work provides a convincing illustration.

In other words, the direction of movement has been up the levels of the linguistic system and out at the top. The focus of attention has gone from the phonological system, to the lexicogrammatical system (syntax), to the semantic system, and is now moving out to the cognitive system. In the latest analysis, the learning process is a process of cognitive development and the learning of the mother tongue is an aspect of it and is conditioned by it.

The present discussion shares this non-autonomous approach to language. It seems sensible to assume that neither the linguistic system itself, nor the learning of it by a child, can be adequately understood except by reference to some higher level of semiotic organization. But we have adopted the alternative perspective— one that is complementary to the cognitive one, not contradictory to it—of locating this higher level semiotic not in the cognitive system but in the social system. The social semiotic is the system of meanings that defines or constitutes the culture; and the linguistic system is one mode of realization of these meanings. The child's task is to construct the sytem of meanings that represents his own model of social reality. This process takes place inside his own head; it is a cognitive process. But it takes place in contexts of social interaction, and there is no way it can take place except in these contexts. As well as being a cognitive process, the learning of the mother tongue is also an interactive process. It takes the form of the continued exchange of meanings between the self and others. The act of meaning is a social act.

The social context is therefore not so much an external condition on the learning of meanings as a generator of the meanings that are learnt. And part of the social context is the language that is used by the interactants—the language the child hears around him. It has been concluded from recent semantic interpretations of language development, in the work of Bever, Osgood, Bowerman, and others, that a child learns ideational meanings that reflect the world around him: for example, the distinction between things, on the one hand, and relations between things on the other. One theory is that the whole inventory of transitivity functions is recoverable from the extralinguistic environment; this is suggested for example by Greenfield & Smith's interesting application of Fillmore's 'case theory' to one-word utterances of Phase II. But the structure of the environment, as apprehended by the child, is coded in the mother tongue. Even in Phase I, the semantics of the mother tongue determines the meanings that the mother and others respond to, thus helping to shape the child's social reality. By Phase II, when the child is building a lexicogrammatical system, things and the relations between them are entirely interpreted through the mother tongue; this is an inevitable consequence of having a lexicogrammar—the child is no longer free to code as he likes. (In case this appears as a Whorfian conception, let it be said at once that it is—but in terms of what Whorf said, not of what he is often assumed to have said. We are not the prisoners of our cultural semiotic; we can all learn to move outside it. But this requires a positive act of semiotic reconstruction. We are socialized within it, and our meaning potential is derived from it.) What makes learning possible is that the coding imposed by the mother tongue corresponds to a *possible* mode of perception and interpretation of the environment. A green car *can* be analyzed experientially as carness qualified by greenness, if that is the way the system works.

Important though this is, however, it is still only an aspect of a more significant fact about language and the social system, that which we illustrated in Section 3. The essential condition of learning is the systematic link between semantic categories and the semiotic properties of the situation. The child can learn to mean because the linguistic features in some sense relate to features of the environment. But the environment is a social construct. It does not consist of things, or even of processes and relations; it consists of human interaction, from which the things derive their meaning. The fact that a bus moves is by no means its only or even its most obvious perceptual quality, as compared, say, with its size, its shininess, or the noise it makes; but it is its most important semiotic property, the meaning with which it is endowed in the social system, and it is this that determines its semantic status in English. Things have to be interpreted in their social contexts. More relevant, perhaps, they have to be interpreted in their social *proportion*; they are not that important, so to speak, compared with the processes of interaction themselves.

This is, of course, deliberately to overstate the case. The point being made is that the reality in which meaning takes place is a social reality into which the external environment enters through its significance for interaction, and is embedded in contexts of evaluation, argument, manipulation, and other social acts. Nor is it suggested that the child does not perform his own interpretations of reality and adapt the linguistic system to them; he certainly does. Nigel, for example, like many other children, had in Phase II some meaning such as 'capable of moving by itself', and used the form gó as a general question 'is it alive?' (in the early stages also applied to vehicles); some form of 'animal, vegetable or mineral?' seems to be very generally adopted as a learning strategy. But the semantics of things is only a part of the total semantic system; most of the time when we are talking about things we are relating them to ourselves; and whether we are or not, they have been coded into the system in a way which reflects their relation to, and value for, the social process.

So when we stress the fact that language takes place in a context of situation, and say that a child is able to learn from what he hears because there is a systematic relation between what he hears and what is going on around him, this is not primarily because our talk is focussed on the objects and events of the external world. Much of the time it is not; and even when it is, it does not reflect their structure in any unprocessed or 'objective' way, but as it is processed by the culture. The relation of talk to environment lies in the total semiotic structure of the interaction: the significant ongoing activity (and it is only through this that 'things' enter into the picture, in a very indirect way), and the social matrix within which meanings are being exchanged. The 'situation' of discourse is made up of these two elements, together with a third, the semiotic modes that are being adopted—in other words, the field, tenor, and mode of section 4 above.

The point has been developed by Lois Bloom that the speech of a young child can be understood only by reference to the context of situation, and it can be maintained that language development consists in progressively freeing the system from dependence on situational constraints. But we find that the major step has already been taken by Nigel at the very beginning of Phase II, when he moves from observation to recall (from 'I see cars, buses . . .' to 'I saw cars, buses . . .' said when they are no longer in sight), and from 'I want what is there in front of me' to 'I want (something which I can't see, e.g.) a rusk'. The direct dependence of a speech instance on the perceptual environment disappears the moment he introduces the third level into his system, the lexico-grammatical level of words and structures, since this provides him with an abstract ('formal') level of coding which intervenes between content (the level of reference to the situation) and output. From the time when the child enters the transition to the adult mode his individual speech acts are no longer constrained by features of the immediate situation. But this does not mean, on the other hand, that there is no systematic link between the meanings the child expresses and the environment in which the act of meaning takes place. There is—but so there is also with the adult. The conception of language development as the freeing of the meaning potential from the confines of 'here and now' is a valid one provided we interpret it not in absolute terms but as a *change* in the nature of the relation of meaning to environment. We have in fact already identified the conditions for this change, when we show the progressive evolution of the concept of 'function' from a stage (Phase I) where it is synonymous with 'use', at which therefore meaning relates directly to the immediate situation, to a stage (Phase III) where it is equivalent to 'component of the semantic system', at which meaning relates to the situation only indirectly, through the social semiotic—the socially constructed reality and the place accorded to language within it. Note that the former is a characterization of Phase I, before the child has embarked on learning what we recognize as language—that is, an adult-like system. At the beginning of Phase II, when 'function' is becoming generalized and conventional linguistic forms—words and structures—are starting to appear, 'constraint' by, or dependence on, the situation already takes the more abstract form of the selective association of meanings with the different social values accorded to the environment, either as terrain to be explored (mathetic) or as mineral to be quarried (pragmatic). There is no restriction such that words and structures can be used to name only what is in sight; what there is, as we have seen, is a tendency for each word, and each structure, to be activated in one function only—certain words and structures in a pragmatic function, other words and structures in a mathetic function. By the time we reach Phase III, the dependence of meaning on context has been reinterpreted at a still more abstract level, although it is still the same general principle at work. In Phase III, and in adult language generally, there is a tendency for each functional component in the meaning potential to be activated by a corresponding component in the context of situation. At no stage is meaning totally context-bound, and equally, at no stage is it totally unrelated to the context; but 'context' means different things at different stages. The Phase I functional headings specify meaning and context undifferentially: a term like 'instrumental' covers both. In Phase III the 'functions' are ways of meaning, and we have to find other frames of reference to characterize the situation as a social construct. It is worth observing, however, that even at Phase I the context of situation is a social construct and its elements are defined by social value: an object is a favourite object, a person is a mother. At no time does the environment in which meaning takes place consist solely of 'props', of the uninterpreted sights and sounds of the material world. Even at nine months, the 'things' to which the child's meanings relate realize values in his social system.

Meaning is at the same time both a component of social action and a symbolic representation of the structure of social action. The semiotic structure of the environment—the ongoing social activity, the roles and statuses, and the interactional channels— both determines the meanings exchanged and is created by and formed out of them. This is why we understand what is said, and are able to fill out the condensations and unpeel the layers of projection..It is also why the system is permeable, and the process of meaning subject to pressures from the social structure. The particular modes and patterns of meaning that tend to be associated with different types of social context are determined by the culture, through a process that Bernstein has interpreted and referred to by the term 'codes'. The reality that the child constructs is that of his culture and sub-culture, and the ways in which he learns to mean and to build up registers—configurations of meanings associated with features of the social context—are also those of his culture and sub-culture. He builds the semiotic of his own society, through interaction in family, in peer group, and, later, in school—as well as in a host of other microsemiotic encounters which, though outside the main socializing agencies, may for that very reason be relatively even more foregrounded in their effects. But at this point we must leave the story, to take it up from another vantagepoint elsewhere. We conclude with a final section showing Nigel on the eve of his second birthday, busily meaning from the moment he wakes up.

7. Over the threshold: Nigel at the end of NL 10

(Early morning. N. comes into F.'s study.)
N. Where the little chùffa . . . you want the little green chuffa that you found on the pàvement

(Garbage lorry draws up outside)
F. Do you want to see the garbage lorry?
N. Find the little green chúffa

(N. runs out to M.)
N. Have your big chúffa (M. gives it to him) . . . it got bènt . . . it not bent nǒw . . . it was broken yěsterday but Daddy had to mend it with a scrèwdriver . . . We must rèady to go on a tràin (repet.)
M. No, we're not going on a train, not today. When we go to Claremont, first we're going on a train and then on an aeroplane.
N. Not going on tràin . . . (starts looking at book) . . . That was a big tràin . . . that was an òld train . . . they've taken awày that train . . . it doesn't go any mòre . . . it got a tall chìmney . . . that was a very òld train . . . might go and see that tràin one dáy . . . and we might go and see that old tràin one dáy (repet.) . . . we will walk on the ràilway line (2) . . . look at the train with the tiny tiny stàr on . . . now that is the light shining out of the train on to the plàtform . . . now that is a very fast tràin and it say whòosh . . . if that train coming past (whispers) and it say whòosh . . . that a fast whòosh train . . . the train say whòosh (2) . . . (finishes the book) . . . But first on to the tráin . . . first on to the blue tráin . . . and then on an àeroplane . . . but we don't go thǎt way

(N. comes back into F.'s study)
N. Gárbage lorry (4) (looking out of window)
F. Has it gone?
N. Want your green pén (2) . . . when Daddy finished writing with that pen and thèn you can have Daddy green pén . . .

Daddy wòrking . . . make cross on týpewriter . . . we have to put
some pàper ín it

(F. puts paper in typewriter. N. strikes keys)
F. What did you make?
N. A dòt . . . (several characters come up together and stick) . . .
Put that dówn . . . yes you will put that dówn

(N. presses down, gets fingers inky; is taken to have fingers
wiped, returns to typewriter)
N. (strikes key; indicating mark on paper) What thàt
F. That's called a caret.
N. 'm putting them all dòwn . . . that one make a ǹkuwa
('stick') . . . a ràɪlway line . . . want to have your green pén

(N. strikes keys again; two characters stick)
N. That twò (3)

(N. listens to F.'s watch)
N. Daddy clock going ticktockticktòck . . . shall we—. . . shall
we make a church spíre (2) . . . with a goglgò ('weathercock') ón
it . . . have you màde a church spíre (2) ('look I've made a church
spire!') . . . thère the gogogogó . . . have the red pén (2) . . . have
Daddy red pén . . . (drops green pen) what did you dròp?
F. I don't know; what did you?
N. Did you drop the green pén ('I dropped the green pen')
(F. picks it up) . . . chúffa . . . draw a chúffa . . . put it báck . . .
shall we make a railway line with the red pén . . . shall we make a
railway line with the chùffa ón it
F. All right, let's make a railway line.
N. Shall we make a fast train which say whóosh, sháll we . . .
(F. & N. drawing) . . . Daddy said I wonder that penguin will
dive in the wàter . . . shall we make a pénguin . . . (F. draws
penguin) . . . it gó . . . gó . . . gó ('is it alive?') . . . ? we drawn a?
fast weel tràin ('fast diesel train')
F. No its an electric train; its got a pantograph.
N. It an elèctric train . . . it got a pàntograph

╲falling tonic (adult tone 1)
╱rising tonic (adult tone 2 or 3)
╲╱ falling-rising tonic (adult tone 4)

	Instrumental	Regulatory	Interactional	Personal	Heuristic	Imaginative	Informative	TOTAL
Phase I								
NL 1 (9–10½ mo.)	2	2	3	5	—	—	—	12
NL 2 (10½–12 mo.)	3	2	7	9	—	—	—	21
NL 3 (12–13½ mo.)	5	6	7	9	—	2	—	29
NL 4 (13½–15 mo.)	5	6	7	11	(?)	3	—	32
NL 5 (15–16½ mo.)	10	7	15	16	(?)	4	—	52
Phase II								
NL 6 (16½–18 mo.)	31	29	16	61*	3	5	—	145

Table 1

* Note: this figure includes all expressions used in observation and recall, reinterpreted in Phase II as 'mathetic' (deriving from personal-heuristic).

148

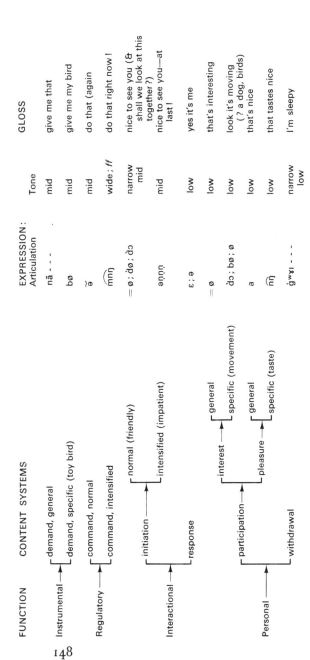

FUNCTION	CONTENT SYSTEMS	EXPRESSION: Articulation	Tone	GLOSS
Instrumental	demand, general	nã - - -	mid	give me that
	demand, specific (toy bird)	bø	mid	give me my bird
Regulatory	command, normal	ə̃	mid	do that (again
	command, intensified	m̃n̄n̄	wide; ff	do that right now !
Interactional	initiation — normal (friendly)	ə ; dọ ; dọ	narrow mid	nice to see you (& shall we look at this together?)
	initiation — intensified (impatient)	ənṇn̄	mid	nice to see you—at last!
	response — general	e ; ɜ	low	yes it's me
	response — specific (movement)	ø	low	that's interesting
		dọ ; bø ; ø	low	look it's moving (? a dog, birds)
Personal	participation — general	a	low	that's nice
	participation — specific (taste)	n̄m̄	low	that tastes nice
	withdrawal	ġʷɐɪ - - -	narrow low	I'm sleepy

Figure 1. NL 1: Nigel at 0; 9–0; 10½

Note: All above on falling tone; mid = mid fall, narrow low = low fall over narrow interval, &c. Similarly in Figure 2, except where otherwise shown.

At 0; 9, Nigel had two such meanings, both expressed as [ø] on mid or mid-low falling tone; one interactional, "let's be together", the other (usually with the wider interval) personal, "look, it's moving". He also had another three meanings expressed gesturally: two instrumental, "I want that", grasping object firmly, and "I don't want that", touching object lightly; and one regulatory, "do that again", touching person or relevant object firmly (e.g. "make that jump in the air again"). The gestures disappeared during NL 1–2.

In this and subsequent Figures, favourite items are indicated by *, and rare or doubtful items by ?. Where two or three items are related in both meaning and sound these are shown by =, accompanied by an index number where necessary. - - - indicates that the syllable is repeated. (-), (- -) indicate typical number of optional repetitions.

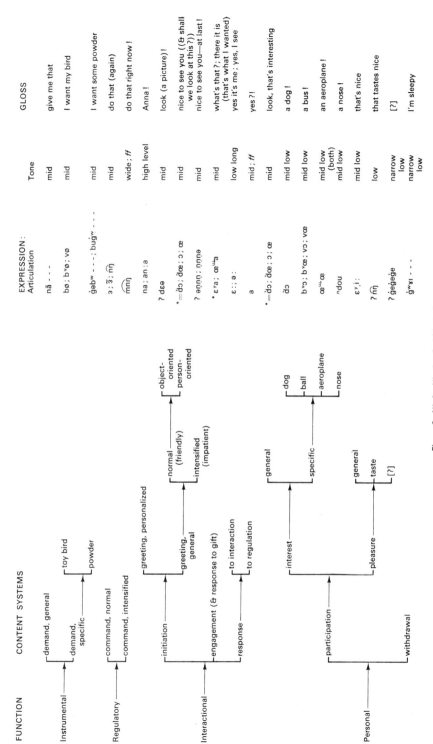

Figure 2. NL 2: Nigel at 0; 10½–1; 0

149

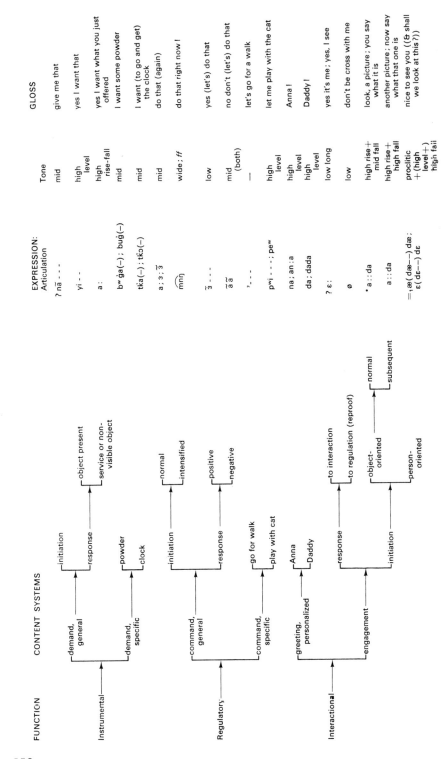

FUNCTION	CONTENT SYSTEMS	EXPRESSION: Articulation	Tone	GLOSS
Instrumental	demand, general — initiation / response (object present / service or non-visible object)	ʔ nã - - -	mid	give me that
		yi - -	high level	yes I want that
		a:	high rise-fall	yes I want what you just offered
	demand, specific (powder / clock)	bʷ ġa(–); buġ(–)	mid	I want some powder
		tka(–); tkɔ(–)	mid	I want (to go and get) the clock
Regulatory	command, general — initiation / response (normal / intensified)	a; ɔ; ɔ̃	mid	do that (again)
		m̂nŋ	wide; ff	do that right now I
	command, specific (positive / negative)	ɜ - - -	low	yes (let's) do that
		ã a	mid (both)	no don't (let's) do that
	(go for walk / play with cat)	ʔ - - -	—	let's go for a walk
		pʷi - - -; peʷ	high level	let me play with the cat
Interactional	greeting, personalized (Anna / Daddy)	na; an:a	high level	Anna I
		da; dada	high level	Daddy I
	engagement — response (to interaction / to regulation (reproof))	ʔ ɛ:	low long	yes it's me; yes, I see
		ø	low	don't be cross with me
	engagement — initiation (object-oriented (normal / subsequent) / person-oriented)	*a::da	high rise + mid fall	look, a picture; you say what it is
		a::da	high rise + high fall	another picture; now say what that one is
		=i,æ(dæ—)dæ; ɛ(dɛ—)dɛ	proclitic + (high level+) high fall	nice to see you ((ɛ shall we look at this?))

150

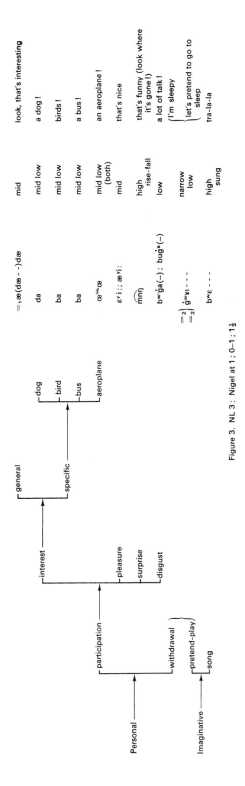

general	┌ dog	=₁æ(dæ - -)dæ	mid	look, that's interesting
		da	mid low	a dog !
	├ bird	ba	mid low	birds !
specific	├ bus	ba	mid low	a bus !
	└ aeroplane	œᵚœ	mid low (both)	an aeroplane !
interest		ɛˠi:; æˠi:	mid	that's nice
		m͡nn	high rise-fall	that's funny (look where it's gone !)
		bᵚˑga(–); bugᵃ(–)	low	a lot of talk !
pleasure				(I'm sleepy
surprise		=₂) ġᵚxi - - -	narrow	let's pretend to go to
disgust		=₂)	low	sleep
participation		bᵚɛ - - - -	high sung	tra-la-la

Personal ── participation ┬ interest ┬ general ┬ dog / bird / bus / specific ─ aeroplane

Imaginative ── ┬ pretend-play / song

Figure 3. NL 3: Nigel at 1; 0–1; 1½

151

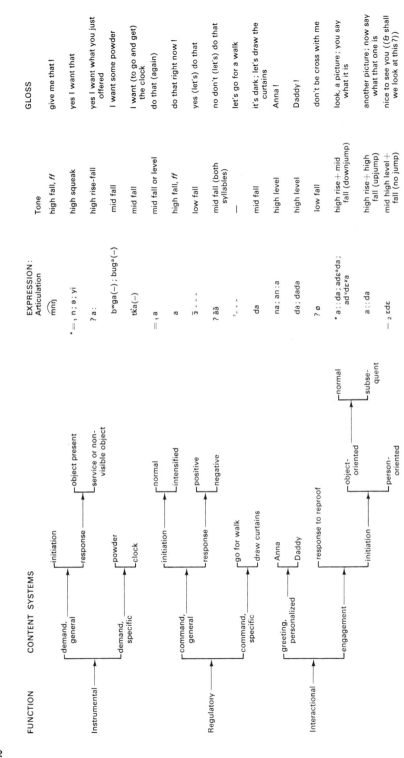

FUNCTION	CONTENT SYSTEMS	EXPRESSION: Articulation	Tone	GLOSS
Instrumental	demand, general — initiation	(m̄n̄)	high fall, ff	give me that I
	demand, general — response — object present	* ≡₁ n ː ə ; yi	high squeak	yes I want that
	demand, general — response — service or non-visible object	ʔ a ː	high rise-fall	yes I want what you just offered
	demand, specific — powder	bʷga(–) ; bugᵃ(–)	mid fall	I want some powder
	demand, specific — clock	tˈka(–)	mid fall	I want (to go and get) the clock
Regulatory	command, general — initiation — normal	≡₁ a	mid fall or level	do that (again)
	command, general — initiation — intensified	a	high fall, ff	do that right now I
	command, general — response — positive	ã - - -	low fall	yes (let's) do that
	command, general — response — negative	ʔ ãã	mid fall (both syllables)	no don't (let's) do that
	command, specific — go for walk	ˈ - - -	—	let's go for a walk
	command, specific — draw curtains	da	mid fall	it's dark; let's draw the curtains
Interactional	greeting, personalized — Anna	na ; an ː a	high level	Anna !
	greeting, personalized — Daddy	da ; dada	high level	Daddy !
	engagement — response to reproof	ʔ ø	low fall	don't be cross with me
	engagement — initiation — object-oriented — normal	* a ː ː da ; adɛᵊda ; adˈdɛˠa	high rise + mid fall (downjump)	look, a picture ; now say what it is
	engagement — initiation — object-oriented — subsequent	a ː ː da	high rise + high fall (upjump)	another picture ; now say what that one is
	engagement — initiation — person-oriented	≡₂ ɛdɛ	mid high level + fall (no jump)	nice to see you ((ɛ shall we look at this?))

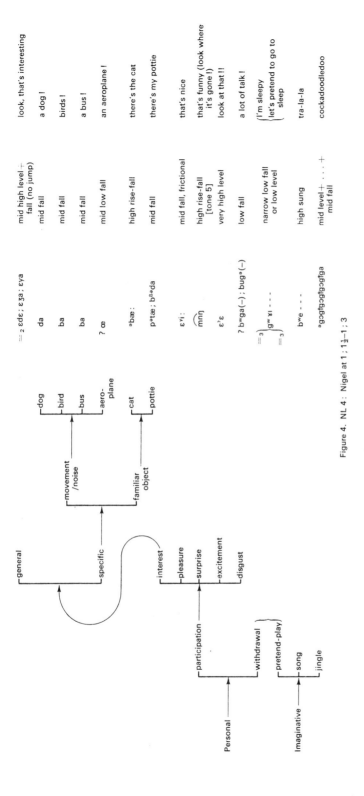

Figure 4. NL 4: Nigel at 1 : 1½–1 ; 3

153

FUNCTION	CONTENT SYSTEMS				EXPRESSION: Articulation	Tone	GLOSS
Instrumental	demand, general	initiation	normal		m	short high fall, ff	give me that
			exploratory		aˀa	mid level+ high level	that's new ; let me see it
		response	plaintive		ɛ:he	mid level+ mid low level	somebody do something
			general		n; ə; yi	high squeak	yes I want that
	demand, specific	food	general		afia	mid level+ mid fall	where's my food ?
			specific	rusk	ωɹωɔ	proclitic+ mid fall	I want a rusk
				toast	dɔωba	mid fall over 2 sylls.	I want some toast
		ritual object	powder		bʷga	proclitic+ mid fall	I want the powder
			clock		tɪkᵗtokə	mid fall	I want the clock
		pottie			pəta	proclitic+ mid fall	I want my pottie
Regulatory	command, general	initiation	normal		a; ə	mid fall or level	do that (again)
			intensified		a	high fall, ff	do that right now
		response			ɜ; ɜ; m	low fall	yes (let's) do that
	command, specific	suggestion (joint)	go for walk		ˀ - - -	—	let's go for a walk
			draw picture		dɔə	mid fall	let's draw a picture
		request	draw curtains		da; ɛ:da	(mid rise+) mid fall	it's dark ; draw the curtains
			come for lunch		la	mid fall	come & have your lunch
Interactional	greeting	general	initiation		aloʷwa; aloʷba	mid level+ low rise + mid level or rise	hullo
			response		a:	high level	and hullo to you
		specific			ˀbæ:	high rise-fall	hullo cat
		personalized	Anna		an:a	(see next system)	Anna
			Mummy		ama		Mummy
			Daddy		dada		Daddy
		seeking			(intonation of name)	mid-high level+ high level	where are you ?
		finding			(intonation of name)	mid fall+ low level	there you are
		to 'say "…"!'			miˀ	mid narrow fall	[sole response whatever he is asked to say]

Figure 5 (table)

[Heuristic]			ʔaˀ	slow high fall, glottalized	let's be sad; it's broken, come off
	initiation	normal	aːːda; adˠ(——)da	mid rise or step up + fall (no jump)	look, what's that?
		subsequent	aːːda	mid rise or step up + fall (upjump)	and what's that?
	shared attention				
	movement/noise	dog	da	mid fall	a dog
		bird	ba	mid fall	birds
		bus	ba; aba	mid fall	a bus
		car	kˠa	mid fall	a car
	observation	aeroplane	œ	low fall	an aeroplane
		ball	ba	mid fall	there's my ball
	familiar object	stick	tɪkᵊ	mid fall	there's my stick
		teddy	tɛda	mid fall	there's my teddy
Personal	interest		ɛdɛ	mid high level + fall (no jump)	that's interesting
	pleasure		yi	high rise	that's nice
	surprise		da	high rise-fall	that's funny
	excitement		ɛˀɛ	very high level	look at that
	expression of feeling	favourite object or picture	m	high rise-fall	that's my best...
	ritual joy	mirror	ᵊyiː	proclitic + slow high fall	that's me there
	warning		ɜ: .	mid fall, slow	careful, it's sharp (rough, &c.)
	complaint		ᵊβɛʊ - - -	mid narrow fall	I'm fed up
	game-play	peep-o	ɛː	high rise	peep-o
		hunt the...	ᵊdida	proclitic + mid level + high fall	I've hidden it
Imaginative	play	pretend-play	gˠˣɪ - - -	narrow low fall or level	let's pretend to go to sleep
	jingle		ᵊgɔgl - - ga	mid level + ... + mid fall	cockadoodledoo

Figure 5. NL 5: Nigel at 1; 3–1; 4½

Note: Here there occurs for the first time a set of options which do not form a simple taxonomy. The personal names Anna, Daddy, Mummy combine either with stepping up high level tone, meaning 'where are you?' I'm locking for you,' or with mid fall plus low level tone, meaning 'hullo, there you are!' This involves a level of coding intermediate between content and expression.

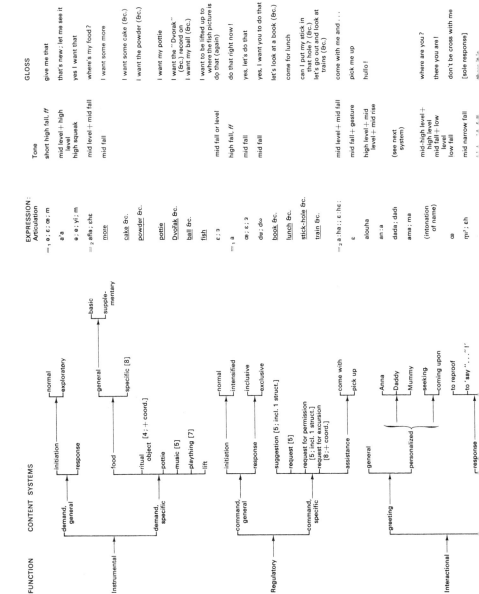

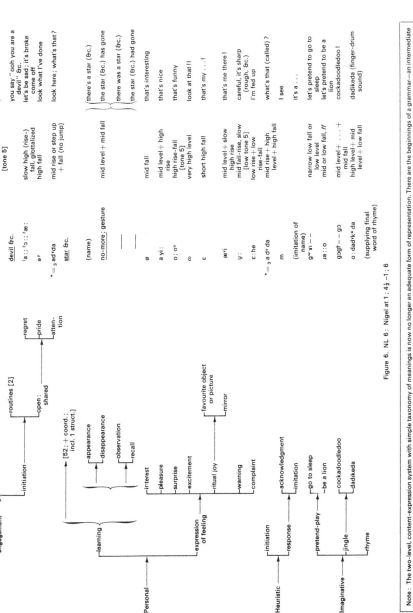

Figure 6. NL 6: Nigel at 1 : 4½ –1 ; 6

Note: The two-level, content-expression system with simple taxonomy of meanings is now no longer an adequate form of representation. There are the beginnings of a grammar—an intermediate level of vocabulary and structure; and meanings are beginning to be combined; (e.g. observation of an object and demand for it). These developments had already been anticipated in NL 5 and even earlier. In the present version, however, for the sake of continuity, NL 6 is shown as if it was still the same kind of system as all those that preceded it.

Figures in square brackets indicate the number of single words occurring as options under the particular heading; "+ coord." indicates that these words also occur in coordination. "incl. 1 struct." indicates that one of the options is expressed by means of a structure (e.g. stick-hole "can I put my stick in that hole?"). Under each such heading, just one word is given, by way of example, and it is cited in orthography; phonetic transcription is used only for those expressions which are not vocabulary items.

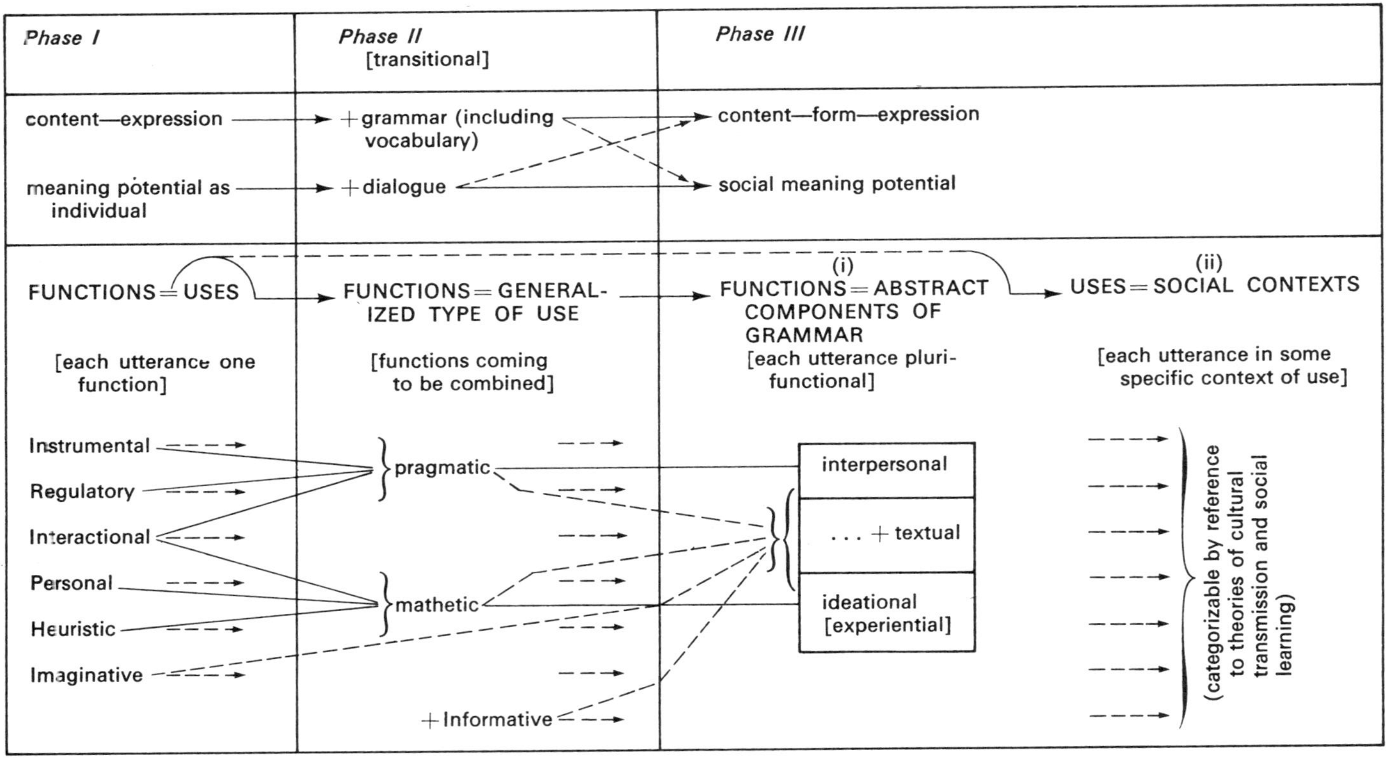

Phase I | Phase II [transitional] | Phase III

content——expression ———→ +grammar (including vocabulary) ——→ content—form—expression

meaning potential as individual ——→ +dialogue ——→ social meaning potential

FUNCTIONS = USES ——→ FUNCTIONS = GENERAL-IZED TYPE OF USE ——→ (i) FUNCTIONS = ABSTRACT COMPONENTS OF GRAMMAR [each utterance pluri-functional] ——→ (ii) USES = SOCIAL CONTEXTS

[each utterance one function]

[functions coming to be combined]

[each utterance in some specific context of use]

(categorizable by reference to theories of cultural transmission and social learning)

interpersonal

... + textual

ideational [experiential]

pragmatic

mathetic

Instrumental
Regulatory
Interactional
Personal
Heuristic
Imaginative

+ Informative

Figure 7. The original developmental functions evolve, at one level, via generalized categories of meaning, into the abstract functional components of the linguistic system; and, at another level, into the social contexts of linguistic interaction.

Bibliography

Bach, Emmon, & Harms, Robert T. (eds.). *Universals in Linguistic Theory.* New York: Holt, Rinehart & Winston, 1968.

Berger, Peter L., & Luckmann, Thomas. *The Social Construction of Reality: a treatise in the sociology of knowledge.* London: Allen Lane (The Penguin Press), 1967.

Berger, Peter L., & Kellner, Hansfried. "Marriage and the construction of reality" Diogenes 46, 1964. Also in Dreitzel (ed.), 1970.

Bernstein, Basil. *Class, Codes and Control I: theoretical studies towards a sociology of language.* London: Routledge & Kegan Paul (Primary Socialization, Language, & Education), 1971.

Bernstein, Basil (ed.). *Class, Codes and Control II: applied studies towards a sociology of language.* London: Routledge & Kegan Paul (Primary Socialization, Language, & Education), 1973.

Bever, Thomas G. "The cognitive basis of linguistic structure" In Hayes (ed.), 1970.

Birk, David. "You never speak a dead language" In Thornton, Birk & Hudson, 1973.

Bloom, Lois M. *Language Development: form and function in emerging grammars.* Cambridge, Mass.: M. I. T. Press (Research Monographs 59), 1970.

Bloom, Lois M. "Language development" In Horowitz et al. (eds.), in press.

Bloom, Lois M. *One Word at a Time: the use of single-word utterances before syntax.* The Hague: Mouton, 1973.

Bowerman, Melissa. *Learning to Talk: a cross-linguistic study of early syntactic development, with special reference to Finnish.* Cambridge: Cambridge U. P., 1973.

Braine, Martin D. S. "The ontogeny of English phrase structure: the first phase" Language 39, 1963.

Braine, Martin D. S. "The acquisition of language in infant and child" In Reed (ed.), 1971.

Britton, James N. *Language and Learning*. London: Allen Lane (The Penguin Press), 1970.

Brown, Roger. *A First Language: the early stages*. Cambridge, Mass.: Harvard U. P., 1973.

Brown, Roger, Cazden, Courtney, & Bellugi, Ursula. "The child's grammar from one to three" In Hill (ed.), 1969.

Buhler, Karl. *Sprachtheorie: die Darstellungsfunktion der Sprache*. Jena: Fischer, 1934.

Bullowa, Margaret. "The start of the language process" *Actes du X Congrès International des Linguistes (Bucharest 1967)*. Bucharest, 1970.

Bush, Clara N. *On the Use of the IPA in Transcribing Child Language: a theoretical orientation and methodological approach*. Stanford, California: Stanford University Committee on Linguistics, Child Language Research Project, in press.

Chukovsky, Kornei. *From Two to Five*. Translated & edited by Miriam Morton. Berkeley, Los Angeles & London: University of California Press, 1971.

Clark, Eve V. "What's in a word? on the child's acquisition of semantics in his first language" In Moore (ed.), in press.

Doughty, Peter S., Pearce, John J., & Thornton, Geoffrey M. *Exploring Language*. London: Edward Arnold, 1972.

Douglas, Mary. "Do dogs laugh? a cross-cultural approach to body symbolism" Journal of Psychosomatic Research 15, 1971.

Dreitzel, Hans Peter (ed.). *Recent Sociology II: patterns of communicative behavior*. New York: Macmillan, 1970.

Elkind, D., & Favell, J. (eds.). *Studies in Cognitive Development*. New York: Oxford U. P., 1969.

Enkvist, Nils Erik, Spencer, John, & Gregory, Michael. *Linguistics and Style*. London: Oxford U. P. (Language & Language Learning 6), 1964.

Ervin, Susan M., & Miller, Wick R. "Language development" In Stevenson (ed.), 1963.

Ervin-Tripp, Susan M. "Social dialects in developmental sociolinguistics" In Shuy (ed.), n.d.

Ervin-Tripp, Susan M. *Language Acquisition and Communicative Choice. Essays selected and introduced by Anwar S. Dil*. Stanford, California: Stanford U. P., 1973.

Ferguson, Charles A., & Slobin, Dan I. (eds.). *Studies of Child Language Development*. New York: Holt, Rinehart & Winston, 1973.

Fillmore, Charles J. "The case for case" In Bach & Harms (eds.), 1968.

Firth, J. R. "Personality and language in society" The Sociological Review 42, 1950. Also in J. R. Firth, *Papers in Linguistics 1934–1951*. London: Oxford U. P., 1957.

Firth, J. R. "A synopsis of linguistic theory" *Studies in Linguistic Analysis* (Special Volume of the Philological Society). Oxford: Blackwell, 1957. Also in Palmer (ed.), 1968.

Greenfield, Patricia Marks, & Smith, Joshua H., *Communication and the Beginnings of Language: the development of semantic structure in one-word speech and beyond.* New York: Academic Press, in press.

Gruber, J. S. "Topicalization in child language" *Foundations of Language* 3, 1967.

Halliday, M. A. K. "Language structure and language function" In Lyons (ed.), 1970.

Halliday, M. A. K. *Explorations in the Functions of Language.* London: Edward Arnold (Explorations in Language Study), 1973.

Halliday, M. A. K. *Language and Social Man.* London: Longman (Schools Council Programme in Linguistics & English Teaching, Papers Series II, 3), 1974.

Halliday, M. A. K., McIntosh, Angus & Strevens, Peter. *The Linguistic Sciences and Language Teaching.* London: Longman (Longmans Linguistics Library), 1964.

Hasan, Ruqaiya. "Code, register and social dialect" In Bernstein (ed.), 1973.

Hayes, J. R. (ed.). *Cognition and the Development of Language.* New York: Wiley, 1970.

Hill, J. P. (ed.). *1967 Minnesota Symposia on Child Psychology.* Minneapolis, Minnesota: University of Minnesota Press, 1969.

Hinde, R. A. (ed.). *Non-Verbal Communication.* Cambridge: Cambridge U. P., 1972.

Hjelmslev, Louis. *Prolegomena to a Theory of Language.* Translated by Francis J. Whitfield. Madison, Wisconsin: University of Wisconsin Press, 1961.

Horowitz, F., Hetherington, E., Scarr-Salapatek, S., & Siegel, G. (eds.). *Review of Child Development Research IV.* Chicago: University of Chicago Press, in press.

Huxley, Renira & Ingram, Elisabeth (eds.). *Language Acquisition: models and methods.* London & New York: Academic Press, 1971.

Hymes, Dell H. "Models of interaction of language and social setting" Journal of Social Issues 23, 1967.

Hymes, Dell H. "Linguistic theory and the functions of speech" *International Days of Sociolinguistics*. Rome: Luigi Sturzo Institute, 1969.

Ingram, David. "Transitivity in child language" Language 47, 1971.

Ingram, Elisabeth. *Psychology and Language Learning*. First unpublished draft.

Jakobson, Roman. "From the point of view of linguistics" International Journal of American Linguistics 19 (Supplement to Vol. 19 no. 2), 1953.

Jakobson, Roman. "Verbal communication" Scientific American, September 1972.

Kelley, K. L. *Early Syntactic Acquisition*. Santa Monica, California: The RAND Corporation, 1967.

Lamb, Sydney M. "Discussion" In Parret, 1974.

Lenneberg, Eric. *Biological Foundations of language*. New York: Wiley, 1967.

Leopold, Werner F. *Speech Development of a Bilingual Child I–IV*. Evanston & Chicago: Northwestern University, 1939–49.

Letham, Margaret. *A Case Approach to Child Language*. University of Edinburgh M. Litt. Thesis (unpublished), 1970.

Lévi-Strauss, Claude. *The Savage Mind*. London: Weidenfeld & Nicolson, 1966.

Lewis, Michael M. *Infant Speech: a study of the beginnings of language*. London: Routledge & Kegan Paul (International Library of Psychology, Philosophy & Scientific Method), 1936; 2nd ed., enlarged, 1951.

Lyons, John. "Human language" In Hinde (ed.), 1972.

Lyons, John (ed.). *New Horizons in Linguistics*. Harmondsworth: Penguin Books, 1970.

Malinowski, Bronislaw. "The problem of meaning in primitive languages". Supplement I to C. K. Ogden & I. A. Richards, *The Meaning of Meaning*. London: Kegan Paul (International Library of Psychology, Philosophy & Scientific Method), 1923.

Malinowski, Bronislaw. *Coral Gardens and their Magic, Volume II*. London: Allen & Unwin; New York: American Book Co., 1934.

Moore, Terence E. (ed.). *Cognitive Development and the Acquisition of Language*. New York: Academic Press, in press.

Morris, Desmond. *The Naked Ape*. London: Jonathan Cape, 1967.

Nelson, Katherine. "Pre-syntactic strategies for learning to talk" New Haven, Connecticut: Yale University Department of Psychology (mimeographed), 1971.

Osgood, Charles. "Where do sentences come from?" In Steinberg & Jakobovits (eds.), 1971.

Osser, Harry. "Three approaches to the acquisition of language" In Williams (ed.), 1970.

Osser, Harry. "Developmental studies of communicative competence" In Shuy (ed.), n.d.

Palmer, Frank R. (ed.). *Selected Papers of J. R. Firth 1952–1959*. London: Longman (Longmans Linguistics Library), 1968.

Parret, Herman. *Discussing Language*. The Hague: Mouton, 1974.

Piaget, Jean. *Language and Thought of the Child*. Translated by Marjorie Gabain. London: Routledge & Kegan Paul, 1926; 3rd ed., revised & enlarged, 1959.

Piaget, Jean. *The Construction of Reality in the Child*. New York: draft.

Pike, Kenneth L. *Language in Relation to a Unified Theory of the Structure of Human Behavior*. The Hague: Mouton (2nd edition, revised) (Janua Linguarum Series Major 24), 1967.

Reed, Carroll E. (ed.). *The Learning of Language*. New York: Appleton-Century-Crofts, 1971.

Regan, John. *The Beginnings of Conversation*. First unpublished draft.

Sacks, Harvey. "An analysis of the course of a joke's telling in conversation" Irvine, California: University of California, Irvine, School of Social Science (mimeographed), 1973.

Schegloff, Emanuel A. "Sequencing in conversational openings" American Anthropologist 70, 1968.

Schlesinger, I. M. "Production of utterances and language acquisition" In Slobin (ed.), 1971.

Shuy, Roger W. (ed.). *Sociolinguistics: a crossdisciplinary perspective*. Washington, D.C.: Center for Applied Linguistics, n.d.

Sinclair de Zwart, H. "Developmental psycholinguistics" In Elkind & Favell (eds.), 1969.

Slobin, Dan I. (ed.). *The Ontogenesis of Grammar: a theoretical symposium*. New York: Academic Press, 1971.

Steinberg, D. D. & Jakobovits, L. A. (eds.). *Semantics: an interdisciplinary reader in philosophy, linguistics and psychology*. Cambridge: Cambridge U. P., 1971.

Stevenson, H. (ed.). *Child Psychology*. Chicago: The National Society for the Study of Education (Sixty-second Yearbook), 1963.

Thornton, Geoffrey M., Birk, David, & Hudson, Richard A. *Language at Work*. London: Longman (Schools Council Programme in Linguistics & English Teaching, Papers Series II, 1), 1973.

Turner, Geoffrey J. "Social class and children's language of control at age five and age seven" In Bernstein (ed.), 1973.

Ure, Jean & Ellis, Jeffrey. "Register in descriptive linguistics and linguistic sociology" In Villegas (ed.), 1972.

Villegas, Oscar Uribe (ed.). *Las Concepciones y Problemas Actuales de la Sociolinguistica*. Mexico: University of Mexico Press, 1972.

Werner, Heinz, & Kaplan, Bernard. *Symbol Formation*. New York: Wiley, 1963.

Whorf, Benjamin Lee. *Language, Thought and Reality*. Selected writings, edited and with an introduction by John B. Carroll. Cambridge, Mass.: M. I. T. Press, 1956.

Williams, Frederick (ed.). *Language and Poverty: perspectives on a theme*. Chicago: Markham, 1970.